# DATE DUE

| | | | |
|---|---|---|---|
| AP 2 99 | | | |
| | | | |
| AP 23 99 | | | |
| | | | |
| MY 1 02 | | | |
| | | | |
| | | | |
| | | | |
| | | | |
| | | | |
| | | | |
| | | | |
| | | | |
| | | | |
| | | | |
| | | | |
| | | | |
| | | | |
| | | | |
| | | | |
| | | | |

DEMCO 38-296

THE NECESSITY OF EXPERIENCE

K

# The Necessity of Experience

Edward S. Reed

*Yale University Press  New Haven and London*

Designed by Rebecca Gibb. Set in Postscript Monotype Bembo type by Keystone
Typesetting, Inc., Orwigsburg, Pennsylvania. Printed in the United States of America by
Vail-Ballou Press, Binghamton, New York.

Library of Congress Cataloging-in-Publication Data
Reed Edward (Edward S.)
      The necessity of experience / Edward S. Reed.
          p.   cm.
      Includes bibliographical references and index.
      ISBN 0–300–06668–6 (alk. paper)
          1. Experiential learning.    2. Experience—Psychological aspects.
      3. Human information processing.    4. Schemas (Psychology)
      I. Title.
      BF318.5.R44    1996
      128'.4—dc20                                          96–5980
                                                           CIP

"Vientos del pueblo," words and music by Victor Jara, additional lyrics by Miguel
Hernandez. Copyright © 1972 Mighty Oak Music Ltd., London. TRO-Essex Music
International, Inc., controls all publication rights for U.S.A. and Canada. Reprinted by
permission.

A catalogue record for this book is available from the British Library.
The paper in this book meets the guidelines for permanence and durability of the
Committee on Production Guidelines for Book Longevity of the Council on Library
Resources.

10   9   8   7   6   5   4   3   2   1

I dedicate this book to three who took the experience of this century, shaped it into song, and returned it as a gift to the people of our wounded globe:

VICTOR JARA

BOB MARLEY

PETE SEEGER

*Vientos del pueblo me llaman*
*Vientos del pueblo me llevan*
*Me esparacen el corazón*
*Y me avientan la garganta*
*Así cantará el poeta*
*Mientras el alma me suene*
*Por los caminos del pueblo*
*Desde ahora y para siempre.*

Victor Jara

*Our life is not so much threatened as our perception.*

Ralph Waldo Emerson

# CONTENTS

Acknowledgments    ix

Prologue: A Plea for Experience    1

ONE  Have You Ever Been Experienced? Philosophy Meets the Real World    10

TWO  The Search for a Philosophy of Experience    32

THREE  Fear of Uncertainty and the Flight from Experience    51

FOUR  The Degradation of Experience in the Modern Workplace    68

FIVE  Sharing Experience    92

SIX  Experience and Love of Life    117

SEVEN  Experience and the Birth of Hope    133

Epilogue: Fighting for Experience    158

Notes    165

Further Reading    179

Index    185

# ACKNOWLEDGMENTS

This book is one of a trilogy on which I have been working for many years. The other two books are *Encountering the World: Towards an Ecological Psychology* (1996) and *From Soul to Mind: The Emergence of Psychology, 1815–1890* (forthcoming). I wish to thank the John Simon Guggenheim Memorial Foundation for a fellowship in 1994–95 without which I would not have been able to complete these books.

The present book has been written and rewritten in a number of forms over the past decade, and I apologize in advance if I neglect to thank some of the many people who helped me at various stages of the project. For reading several drafts and offering helpful comments: Mike Montgomery, Doug Porpora, Dave and Doug Noble, Harry Heft, Bert Hodges, and Alan Fogel. Stan Gaines and Mike Penn offered useful information and advice about areas of social and personality psychology. A special thanks to Jonathan Cobb, who gave the penultimate draft a scrupulous reading, critique, and editing, enabling me to produce a much better final version of the book. At Yale University Press, Gladys Topkis was always helpful and a pleasure to deal with, and Susan Laity's marvelous editorial work has greatly improved the book.

# PROLOGUE   A Plea for Experience

It is difficult not to be puzzled by the ironies of our so-called information age. The technology for processing and transmitting information has progressed rapidly in recent decades, but in spite of this technological progress there has been considerable regress in meaningful communication among people: a marked rise in nationalism, sectarianism, and violence against persons; increases in ignorance and illiteracy within our "advanced" society; and in many places increases in mindless work, alleviated only by mindless entertainment. Sadly, many of us are doomed to spend much of our work time in this age of information pushing buttons, dragging light beams, and responding like machines to symbols created by someone else, symbols that hold no meaning for us. No wonder so many of us spend our leisure time channel surfing.

As this is written, billions of dollars are being spent to create continent-wide information superhighways along which will flow every conceivable kind of information except one. The information being left out of these developments is, unfortunately, the most important kind: the information—termed *ecological*—that all human beings acquire from their environment by looking, listening, feeling, sniffing, and tasting—the information, in other words, that allows us to *experience things for ourselves.*

Most of our experience of the world comes from using this information in the service of our own goals, on the basis of our own needs and ideals. In any ordinary environment our senses find an abundance of information to work on, by which we make sense of our surroundings and our daily lives. Ecological information is especially important in our experience of other people. Face-to-face interaction is the source of all social relationships, and this interaction is possible only because of the subtle skills in using ecological information that every healthy child acquires in the first year of life. We human beings are extraordinarily acute observers of one another: we can see the subtlest changes in facial expression, hear the slightest inflection of doubt or pain in a voice, notice minute alterations in posture or gestures. Until the advent of telecommunications, all forms of social interaction and regulation were based directly on these remarkable skills of primary experience.

There is nothing intrinsically wrong with processed information. The selection and processing of information, the making of images, signs, and symbols, is an old and important human activity. We love to take our own experience and create from it new forms of information for other people. Pictures, songs, jokes, and stories are essential to human happiness, whether in the form of tales told around the fire or via a television from a satellite dish. But one has to have experiences before they can be shared. Telecommunication works only because people who cannot observe one another directly nevertheless have considerable previous experience with direct, face-to-face interaction. For understanding our place in the world, ecological information is thus primary, processed information secondary. It is this relation between primary and processed experience, in which the balance should be tilted toward primary experience, that has been disrupted and degraded by modern life.

When information is processed—selected, modified, packaged, and presented—it can at best provide *secondhand* or indirect knowledge. If I am looking at a photograph of you instead of looking at your face, there is an inherent *limit* to what I can learn about you. No matter how thoroughly I scrutinize the photograph, at some point I stop learning about you and begin to learn about the picture (its graininess, color, light values). But when I meet you face to face there is no limit to the possibilities of exploration and discovery. There are some people and faces I want to keep experiencing and learning more about for the rest of my life, and I hope this is true for everyone reading this book. It is on firsthand experience—direct contact with things, places, events, and people—that all our knowledge and feeling ultimately rest. The meaning of secondhand experience derives from and is dependent on primary experience. Processed information has value and meaning, but the value and meaning emerge precisely because of the relation between the processed information and its sources, not because of any meaning intrinsic in the processed information itself. I can tell you about the smile I saw when I told her you love her, or you can tell her and observe it yourself. Both cases of communication are meaningful, but there are differences—and real limitations—to indirect experience, to being told about things, as opposed to observing them for oneself.

There is, to repeat, nothing intrinsically wrong with processed information, but there is something wrong with a society that spends so much money—as well as countless hours of human effort—to make the least dregs of processed information available to everyone everywhere and yet does little or nothing to help up us *explore the world for ourselves*. When processed experience becomes dominant, something is terribly wrong, especially in a society that aspires to be democratic. In secondhand experience individual powers of scrutiny eventually reach a limit, after which we must follow a path or idea put there by somebody else. (Exactly how did she smile? Were there subtle messages in the smile?) The less firsthand experience we enjoy, the less likely we are to learn how to profit from our circumstances, to think and feel for ourselves, and to act according to our own lights.

Yet we have organized our world to undermine primary experience. In those activities in particular to which we devote most of our time—work, school, leisure—we now emphasize learning *about* things (using secondhand experience), and we limit our opportunities for primary experience. It is almost as if we had set about to root primary experience out of everyday life. Our educational and vocational practices over the past century have moved from a hands-on, apprenticeship approach to a "user's manual plus question menu" approach. In fields as diverse as art and engineering, business and philosophy, we have been persuaded that learning about things on the basis of processed information—on the basis of what others tell us the thing is about—is an adequate substitute for coming to understand things for ourselves through primary experience. Daily life in our schools and workplaces is increasingly dominated by secondhand experience, and many of the rules in such institutions are specifically designed to limit independent exploration of our environment and independent interaction with others—or both.

Even our sex lives have become processed. Pornography and prostitution are as old as civilization, but only in the postmodern world—beginning with magazines and now extending to videos, computers, and telephone systems—has a mass industry based on secondhand and preprocessed lust flourished. It is no exaggeration to say that millions of orgasms are manufactured daily in a manner divorced from any kind of face-to-face intimacy and reciprocity, whether of love or desire, convenience or profit. No doubt a few people benefit from the distanced intimacy of phone-based relationships; but it is equally certain that most of this sexual activity has had all the meaningful social relating bleached out of it. To the extent that increasingly large portions of our population find intimacy difficult and noninteractive sex normal, we have succeeded in subverting one of the most important aspects of human interaction in approximately a single generation.

In this book I argue that the psychosocial ills that beset many of us today—what historian Eric Hobsbawm calls the increasing barbarism of daily life—stem largely from the degradation of opportunities for primary experience that is rampant in all developed and developing societies. The result of organizing work, school, and leisure to emphasize secondhand experience is a dramatic decrease in the time available for primary experience. Such organization often leads to increasing costs being incurred by individuals who attempt to obtain primary experience. As our opportunities for primary experience shrink in everything from manual and social skills to learning about nature, society, or work, we become increasingly unable to function in the real world. We shelter in the pseudo- and virtual realities created for us by others and take our own paths less and less frequently.

This is especially true when it comes to social dealings. Children whose dominant experience of social interaction derives from viewing television (as opposed to playing with peers or interacting with family members) often turn into odd creatures who play to invisible audiences and cannot connect reliably with the people around them. With some laudable and important exceptions, our schools have taken industrial settings as models for their classes, a move that restricts children from interacting, thus depriving them of opportunities to develop their social and empathic skills; so perhaps it is no surprise that most children spend more than half their waking hours plugged into the processed information box. Children who grow up with relatively little experience in the complex give-and-take of interaction are unlikely to become adept at interacting, much less to find the time or motivation to improve their social skills.

In his posthumously published *Revolt of the Elites,* Christopher Lasch suggests that the psychological root of our current problems is that elite populations, especially in the past half-century, have separated themselves from the majority of the people. This separation is evident in the different interests, patterns of living, and access to social resources of the two groups. Corresponding to this separation, Lasch rightly diagnoses a lack of respect for ordinary, everyday experience as a central tenet in much modern social theory and practice. Social theorists and policy makers have themselves become increasingly concerned with regulating the attitudes and activities of masses of people, leaving fewer avenues open for these people to shape their own patterns of experience and behavior.

Although we like to think of the post–World War II era as an age of democracy and opportunity, few of the major innovations in social institutions or organizations in these years have resulted in more *shared* experience or responsibility. Improvements in the access of individuals to social and economic resources have occurred in the context of increasingly large-scale and stratified social organizations. Nondemocratic institutions—megacorporations, large schools, entertainment conglomerates, and prisons—have begun to fill the available social space, dominating the daily life of individuals and crowding out opportunities for autonomous or grassroots activities and experience. Like Lasch, I am *not* arguing that there is some past golden age of good experience and healthy democracy to which we should return. Sadly, our history reveals a past that has as many problems as the present, albeit different ones. But I am arguing, in accord with Lasch's account, that we can learn from past mistakes and successes and try to shape a more meaningful and psychologically appealing future—one that has room for a genuine democracy of experience and respect among different kinds of people.

Calling attention to these problems—even this analysis of them—is by no means new or wholly original. Variants of these worries have been discussed for more than a century, from the popular speeches of the artist and social reformer William Morris

to the cautionary writings of Hannah Arendt, from the ideas of early regional planners like Lewis Mumford to the theories of more recent social commentators like Harry Braverman or Christopher Lasch. These critiques have always been considered peripheral to intellectual discussion, however, in part because many of them have been limited, focused on particular issues, from architecture and artisanship to social theory. These theorists understood the general implications of their critiques, but the breadth and power of those implications have not been widely appreciated.

The purpose of this book is to bring these critiques to the center, by showing that they all stem from a single root: each is an attempt to defend primary experience. For this analysis to work we must understand the differences between primary and secondhand experience. These were not clarified until the 1960s and 1970s, when the perceptual psychologist James Gibson launched a new kind of psychology, which he called ecological psychology, and which which took as its first challenge the task of explaining how people and animals encounter their surroundings. Unfortunately, those who might be expected to be wisest and most helpful about such matters—our philosophers, psychologists, educators, and social theorists—have, under the influence of out-of-date psychological theories, largely endorsed many of the changes that have moved us away from primary experience. In this book I hope to use the insights afforded by Gibson's ecological psychology to integrate the earlier, partial critiques of modern experience and to offer some prosaic and homely suggestions for how we might begin to defend experience from the forces undermining it.

I shall begin this book by reviewing the origins, motives, and implications of the Western anti-experiential philosophy. The scientific revolution of the seventeenth century perfectly suited an abstract, Cartesian view of experience that effectively

denied the existence of primary experience. After Descartes, Western philosophers and scientists tended to replace the commonsense concepts of experience, wisdom, and know-how with an increasingly technical account of experience as made up of disconnected, subjective, sensory states. Ultimately, Descartes divided experience into isolated mental states and acts of judgment, both considered to be interior, subjective, and separated from the world. Not until a century ago did pragmatists like John Dewey and William James offer a philosophy that explicitly tried to understand the value of everyday experience.

Our separation from experience is by no means purely intellectual, however; it is part of daily life in our culture. Although Descartes's division of experience into two mental aspects (both variants of secondhand experience) might be considered pure intellectual theorizing, the increasing use of technology has brought about a replication of this unhealthy division of experience in many aspects of our daily lives, at our workplaces, schools, and even homes. Like Cartesian philosophers, we now deal almost exclusively in secondhand information.

We need to fight the modern tendency to degrade primary experience and to replace it with restricted and inferior secondhand experience. To do this we must learn to place appropriate emphasis on primary experience without losing sight of the possibilities of improving secondhand experience as well. By locating our analysis within the framework of James Gibson's ecological psychology, we can come to appreciate the value of both kinds of experience and to esteem the special risks we as a society face when we undermine our primary experience. In each of us, hope for the future emerges only from a proper mixture of primary and secondary experience and, as I argue in chapter 7, a rich mixture of the two is needed to foster hope throughout our society. Dewey's insights about the intrinsic connection between democratic education and the potential for growth in experience can help us to see how simple changes in

everyday life—low-tech changes in classrooms, workplaces, or homes—can begin to offer a basis for defending experience.

To fight against the destruction of experience we need to understand the sources of our modern world's penchant for attacking ordinary experience. I argue that our philosophical tradition itself tends to view all everyday experience as degraded, and it is to the origins of these anti-experiential philosophies that I now turn.

# ONE   Have You Ever Been Experienced?
### Philosophy Meets the Real World

The Western philosophical tradition has always been hostile to everyday experience, and this hostility has only intensified with the rise of modern philosophy. After the "new philosophy" associated with the seventeenth-century scientific revolution came to dominate the intellectual world, "serious" Western philosophies began to contain, as a defining feature, an attack on ordinary experience. Indeed, the widely acknowledged first step toward achieving what passes for philosophical wisdom in the West is to debunk much of what nonintellectuals cherish in everyday experience. The scientific and philosophical revolutionaries of the modern world believed that existence consists exclusively of matter and motion; not even color, much less meaning or value, is real. The important experiences of our lives—giving and receiving love, making a home, identifying ourselves with certain activities—are dismissed by mainstream Western thought as unreal: subjective additions to a world that is nothing more than whirling particles. Experience, if it can be said to exist at all, happens only in the mind, and it is not part of the realm of things.

Those theorists who have tried to make a place for something in our world besides matter in motion—a place for love and hate, fear and pride, even color and harmony—have for centuries been labeled naive realists, which is the philosophers' equivalent to tarring, feathering, and running them out of town. Serious philosophers simply do not listen to naive realists, they just get rid of them.

Early in the twentieth century, discontent with this anti-experiential posturing grew stronger, especially in the United States. William James offered his "radical empiricism" as the payoff of pragmatism—a way of bringing philosophy back into contact with human practical reality. James was perhaps the first important philosopher to insist that everyday experience should be the basis for philosophizing. Unlike most Western philosophers, he resisted the assumption that everyday experience was "really" made up of atoms (sensations or ideas in the mind), as everyday objects were supposed to be. James insisted that experience is a complex stream full of currents and eddies, none quite independent of any other. A school of so-called New Realists started from James's radical empiricism and began to reconsider how science, as well as philosophy, could be brought into line with a revitalized concept of experience. The New Realists explicitly rejected Descartes's legacy—the reduction of lived experience to subjective mental atoms—and sought ways to understand the rich history of ordinary experience. At about this time, John Dewey began to develop his metaphysics of experience, in which experience is seen as part of the nature that gives us life.[1]

Unfortunately, all these efforts miscarried. Whenever Jamesians or New Realists tried to answer mainstream epistemologists on their own grounds, they ended up tangled in contradictions or undermining the very richness of the everyday experience they had tried to resuscitate. In awe of physical science, epistemologists assumed that the subjective world must be made up of something akin to "atoms" of experience—but it is difficult, perhaps impossible, to deduce a world worth having out of sensory atoms. The critics demolished the New Realists: Lovejoy slashed and Russell smashed—these realists were naive, they had no way of dealing with illusion or science, and they could not argue their way out of the Cartesian circle. Either individual experience was made up of something like Descartes's private sensory atoms or it wasn't pure experience at all, they insisted. James and his followers asserted that experience could encompass the whole self, perhaps even the whole universe, and this position was attacked as completely misguided. Dewey protested that both the assumptions and the goal of his critics were wrong because these philosophers were forcing us to abandon everyday experience for the peculiar kind found in philosophy books—sensory data, raw feels, neutral logic-phenomenal atoms, and the like. How can these critics know what counts as my experience? he asked. How can they set themselves up, not merely as arbiters of what is real, but as arbiters of what is real for me—or anyone else? But no one responded seriously to Dewey's challenge, and soon mainstream philosophy again became a club with entrance restricted to those who eschewed naive realism and endorsed "the scientific view" of experience.[2]

Now, as the twentieth century is waning, the members of this exclusive club are once again getting restless. Some, like Richard Rorty, want to shut the club down, to do away with a separate discipline of philosophy altogether rather than promulgate false, malicious ideas about experience that impose a single view of reality on everyone. Others have picked up the notion from James and Dewey that one can believe in real, thick, rich experience and still be a philosopher. Maybe, just maybe, the constrictive ideas of the new philosophers of the seventeenth century are finally losing their grip on our culture as we head into the twenty-first century.

But it is sobering to remember that many astute thinkers—from Thomas Reid to Martin Heidegger and Ludwig Wittgenstein—have prematurely declared the demise of anti-experiential philosophy. The mainstream Western philosophical disdain for everyday experience has until now survived all attacks, and a strong defense of that experience has never been sustained. What looks like the beginning of a trend toward a philosophy of genuine experience can thrive only if we are clear about the importance of this trend and if the critique of the anti-experiential philosophy is accompanied by concrete ideas about what a pro-experiential philosophy—something the modern world has never seen—might look like.

### THE OTHERWORLDLY PHILOSOPHERS

The Western philosophical tradition, then, has been from its beginnings an intellectual force for undermining everyday experience. The great Athenian thinkers insisted that there is a gulf between reality and appearance in order to denigrate everyday experience as mere appearance and to emphasize that our experience is never so real as our thoughts. For Plato the abstract idea of a thing—the idea in heaven, as it were—is what is truly real; our world here is but a shadow of that real world. Aristotle had greater respect for experience than Plato, but even he was wedded to a form of essentialist realism that makes it impossible for ordinary experience to be the vehicle of real knowledge. He believed that scientific knowledge had to be a kind of hunt for the hidden essences—secrets—of nature. These essences are not found *in* experience but behind it. For the Greeks, "to know" in any strict sense of the term is to know the forms of things, and one learns about these through everyday experience, not by special processes that lie for the most part outside the realm of ordinary experience.[3]

Although Greek philosophy and its offshoots tended to downgrade experience in the hunt for ideal essences, it took the great scientific revolutionaries of the 1600s to make the destruction of experience a basic tenet of philosophical thinking. First

Galileo insisted that the book of nature was written in the language of mathematics—and, therefore, that ordinary human experience could not decipher the world's meanings. Worse, if the only real things are those that can be counted or analyzed mathematically, then ordinary experience is not a real part of the world. On the heels of this startling concept came a worse one: Descartes, agreeing with Galileo that only what can be mathematized is real, determined to replace ordinary experience with a scientific version, a mathematized account of happenings in the mind and the brain.[4] Western philosophy and science were forced to treat experience as being made up of atoms of the mind because they had determined that only such countable particles were real. To make human experience "real"—in this odd sense of the term—experience had to be redescribed in a way that makes it unrecognizable to most of us. After Descartes, experience and the wisdom or folly to which it might give rise were replaced by the motion of matter in the nervous system and the response of an immaterial rational mind to that motion. The fundamental conceptual innovation that made this switch possible was a radical change in the meaning of *idea*.

To previous Western philosophers, ideas were associated with essences. Platonists thought ideas existed in some quasi-supernatural fashion; Aristotelians looked on them as a kind of natural magic hidden from experience that, for instance, guided the growth of animals and plants into their adult shapes. But after Descartes, ideas became permanently lodged in the human skull, where they were supposed to be the formal intermediaries between the "outside world" and the "inner world."

According to the scientific revolutionaries, all appearances derive from ideas, which in turn derive from the mind's reaction to physical stimulation coming into the nerves. Some thinkers, like Isaac Newton, considered ideas to be little images in the brain; others, Descartes chief among them, saw ideas as the mental "aspects" of motions in the brain. Regardless of these disagreements, all serious "new philosophers" insisted that what we experience consists of these internal ideas, not things in the external world. Thus, when Descartes said, "I think, therefore I am," he did not mean that he had proved that his *body* existed; the "I" that he thought he had proved to exist was his *mind,* his mental state of doubt. From Descartes on, most Western philosophers have convinced themselves that we can experience nothing more than the contents of our own minds: mental states or ideas, things that are radically different from objects in the external world. This disbelief in external things is fundamental to the Western "scientific view" of experience. Given that we can experience only the contents of our own minds, in order to obtain knowledge of the external world, we must take these subjective states and engage in a special kind of thinking. In this new kind of thought, we are supposed to be aware at first only of our subjective states; then, through a recondite process of ratiocination that was never clearly explained, we are said to infer or judge what "must exist" in the outer world to have caused those subjective states. For instance, Descartes claimed that we are first aware of the optical images found at the back of our eyes (or the neural activity caused by those images) and then we infer what caused the image—a friend's face, for example. To learn about the real world, according to this standard philosophical view, the ordinary observer must follow just those special "rules of method," many of which are dismissive of the problems of daily life, that the new philosophers had put forth. Descartes's *Discourse on Method* urges its readers to ignore the upsetting problems of everyday life: the philosopher should conform to the norms of his country so as to have the tranquillity to pursue mental efforts.[5] In this modern Western tradition, deep philosophical questions are supposed to concern such abstract issues as the nature of existence. The everyday, homely issues of how we manage to live our lives have not been considered "basic" or "deep" since Descartes's transformation of philosophy.

After the excitement following Descartes's theories had died down a bit, a sober-minded Scot named Thomas Reid surveyed these developments with ill-concealed horror. In the name of true knowledge and modern science, proponents of ideas (he called it the ideal theory—pun definitely not intended) had seriously undermined common sense and our ordinary understanding of the world. Perhaps an attack on common sense could be justified in developing a scientific theory, he allowed, but how might philosophers justify cutting themselves off from ordinary concerns? Reid's question, first raised in the 1780s, at the height of the Enlightenment, has haunted Western rational thought ever since.[6] Reid's own influence was great, though perhaps not in the form he would have desired. A whole school of "commonsense" philosophers arose that dominated British and American thought for fifty years after Reid. But whereas Reid wished to use common sense to develop philosophical wisdom, much of this school simply wanted to use common sense to attack all forms of intellectual change.

More influential even than this Scotsman was an East Prussian professor of Scottish extraction who in this same decade scandalized the intellectual world with arguments that purported to prove that the new philosophy, for all its scientific pretensions, could not be defended as a science. If knowledge is based on a rational mind interpreting ideas, then we are led, Kant showed, to serious contradictions—antinomies—that cannot be resolved. Kant suggested that we pursue a dual strategy: we should simultaneously adopt empirical realism (embrace ordinary experience as truly informative) and transcendental idealism (not assume that our experience gives us perfect knowledge of things as they are). Kant argued both that our experience is true of the world and that we cannot know the world completely; we had better assume that experience has limitations as well as revelations. Ironically, Kant is probably the most influential modern philosopher—yet not a single important thinker has followed through on both aspects of his suggestion.[7]

This contradiction in the reception of Kant's theory is telling. Philosophers have been unable to take Kant at his literal word. When a sophisticated thinker like Kant says he is an empirical realist, surely he cannot mean what he says! Philosophers always question ordinary experience, don't they? Typically, Kant is taken to mean something almost diametrically opposed to what he says—that he supports some form of empirical idealism, in which the appearances of ordinary experience are shown to deviate from the objects of the external world.[8] The Western tradition is so anti-experience that its proponents can't even hear one of its own most eloquent spokesmen when he defends primary experience.

Most nineteenth-century philosophers who "followed" Kant explicitly rejected his realism for one form of idealism or another. I find it useful to distinguish, very roughly, two alternate metaphysical strands coming out of Kant's thought. In the first, best exemplified by Schopenhauer, primary experience is turned into Kantian "appearances" (as opposed to realities). These appearances are treated not as parts of the real world but as unreal images or plays superimposed upon a reality that is but dimly seen. Schopenhauer explicitly identifies the phenomenal realm with the Indian concept of Maya, a systematic illusion that eternally conceals the nature of reality.[9]

A second metaphysical strand coming out of Kant's worldview is Hegelian theory. Hegel sees the Kantian antinomies not as a kind of logical reductio ad absurdam of the Western metaphysical tradition (which is what Kant says they are) but as proof that the rational soul must undergo internal change. The vehicle for propelling such change will be antinomy: thesis-antithesis and the overcoming of contradictions, which will lead to new stages in thought.[10] In Hegel's view, appearances are always contradictory, but our rational thought contains at least hints for overcoming these contradictions. The way concepts contradict one another, Hegel claimed, helps us develop novel, less contradictory concepts. Thus logic itself may evolve and change, and what was untrue in one time and place may come to be true in other times and places. From the perspective of the earlier new philosophers, Hegel's willingness to postulate internal changes in the soul—in rationality itself—is profoundly troubling. Hegel argued that instead of trying to understand experience when it seems illogical, we need to change how we think of logic. Only a few in the philosophical community were ready to abandon their old logic, even when it seemed to be contradicted by experience. Western philosophers have been quite willing to jettison the world of everyday folks, but many of them were—and are—far less willing to forgo their own conception of an unvarying rationality.

Western philosophy and science are still roughly split between those who agree with Schopenhauer's metaphysics and those who agree with Hegel. For one group, experience delivers only appearances, and reality itself is something far different—whether that be conceptualized in Schopenhauer's terms as will or in modern terms as quantum states or, sometimes, both. For the second group, experience is merely a springboard for our minds, allowing them to move through a series of apparent contradictions and reconciliations. In many cases, this second group of thinkers is forced to identify the universe with the mind, either the mind of God as he unfolds his creation or the human mind. At any rate, for these thinkers there is no reality behind the phenomena, there are only the phenomena and the mind(s) dealing with them.

### THE PRAGMATIC ATTEMPT TO RESCUE EXPERIENCE

With Western thinkers spinning crazily along such paths, it is perhaps no wonder that at the end of the nineteenth century a number of philosophers began to look for an escape from the route previous theorists had taken. Must philosophy be synonymous with disbelief in the everyday world? they wondered. Apparently so, for with few exceptions, this disbelief seemed to be the starting point for Western philosophical reflection. By 1900 a number of quasi-Hegelian and quasi-Schopenhauerian philosophical systems had sprung up across Europe, and they agreed on one point only: their undisguised disdain for primary experience. Increasingly, philosophers interpreted primary experience as being made up of nothing more than mental atoms or sensations; all sorts of mental powers were therefore required if we were to make something meaningful of these sensations.

This was the period in which modern experimental psychology was invented, with its focus on the categorizing of sensations and the timing of mental responses to these (hypothetical) sensations. Psychologists and physiologists began to study factory workers and to interpret their actions and experience entirely in terms of energy release and sensation. Artists painted what they called their "true impressions" of the world, perceptions that were supposedly unsullied by interpretation. Surprisingly, neither the philosophers nor the scientists nor even the artists were deterred by the fact that no one ever seemed to experience either the sensations or the mental powers alleged to be necessary for interpreting those sensations. The worker shoveling coal into a Bessemer furnace is not, in fact, receiving sensations of weight and effort that he then interprets as shovelfuls of coal. He is shoveling coal, real coal, and experiencing just that: great effort in a hot and filthy place. The philosopher's concept of sensation might be a clever way to describe something in a psychologist's laboratory, but it has little relevance elsewhere. Yet to be successful as "professionals" the new scientific psychologists had to show that what they knew and what they did went beyond the purview of common sense. Because of their need to strike out on a path away from everyday experience, their theories, starting in the 1860s, contained descriptions of hypothetical, "unconscious" mental processes: sensations we "did not notice" were said to be linked by unconscious associative and ratiocinative processes to memories we forgot we had.[11]

Perhaps nothing is more indicative of how far removed philosophical theorizing was from ordinary experience than the new schools of painting that were based on trying to get original, unfiltered impressions down on canvas. Doubtless the advent of the camera and the early experiments in motion pictures had much to do with the new way of thinking about painting. That such highly skilled observers and visualizers as painters could be so influenced by "scientific" theories of seeing that *undermined* the ordinary processes of observation is incredible. Nevertheless, many European painters from about 1850 on—and especially such technically oriented artists as the pointillists—happily subscribed to a theory that claimed that one's vision of something happened literally in the blink of an eye (like a camera with a shutter). When the process of looking is reduced to a "snapshot," then the visual world does begin to resemble many impressionist canvasses, with a clearer center than periphery and a swirling array of hues in which each patch of color is rather small.

Edouard Manet's 1874 picture of Claude Monet sitting in a boat and painting, for example, shows a fairly clear image of Monet's face and hat, but his hands are intentionally blurred, and the background scenery is merely sketched in with broad strokes of color and shape. Many Renoir canvasses of large scenes take this form as well. Yet unless one is trying to become a camera, this is not the visual world of everyday experience—it is the scientist's "image on the retina" turned right side up and put on canvas. But we never see the image on our retina because we look at things by moving our eyes and heads, thus viewing the whole scene, not mere impressions. Nevertheless, the impressionist is willing to assert that everyone receives pure sensations that are just little daubs of colored light, registered unconsciously and interpreted (some would say distorted) by further judgments, also unconscious.

At the end of the nineteenth century, with the rise of scientific psychology and the refinements of Western metaphysics mentioned above, intellectuals, scientists, and even artists were literally re-creating experience, trying to redefine and reconstitute it according to their theories. If primary experience did not fit into their theories, they ignored it and hypothesized unconscious experiences to replace it. This effort pushed everyday experience farther to the margins of intellectual life. In the guise of offering rational and scientific analyses of experience, modernists in various fields were subverting experience and substituting for it something entirely different, a thing of their own creation.

Perhaps the most disturbing result of the modernist subversion of experience is its implicit disdain for the everyday. "Experience" used to mean whatever wisdom one managed to gather in the course of one's daily life, but it has increasingly come to be seen as something outside of the everyday, as something exotic. To become experienced in the modern sense one needs to be an adventurer, as immortalized in the Jimi Hendrix song from which this chapter takes its title. We are now so accustomed to the idea of everyday life as boring, bland, routinized, and empty that the earlier concept of experience—found, for example, in Montaigne or Shakespeare, who treat experience as the distillation of everyday life into wisdom—seems alien.[12] But this equation of experience with the exotic is a disaster, psychologically, morally, and philosophically. If experience can be gained only in unusual situations, it becomes the preserve of the hero or the specialist, and wisdom is transformed into mere expertise. From this distorted perspective, we may no longer view even the individual with decades of painfully acquired firsthand knowledge or skill as experienced or wise (we call his wisdom intuitive skill, for example, not real understanding). The Byronic hero and the heroic scientist, products of this separation, make thrilling models, but ultimately the separation of experience from everyday life means that fewer people will be in a position to develop their own experience into wisdom.

As we have seen, the American rebellion against these attacks on experience was spearheaded by William James, first in his psychology and then in his philosophy of pragmatism. James and, later (and more explicitly), Dewey argued that modern philosophy's alliance with the atomistic and reductionistic worldview promoted by the scientific revolution was its Achilles' heel.[13] Forced by its alliance with physical science to dismiss most human experience as subjective froth, this philosophy became increasingly alienated from human concerns. Even an answer to the great philosophical question of the modern era—How can we know the external world?—would not be accounted wisdom by most ordinary folk. But shouldn't philosophy's mission be to help us understand our lives and perhaps even deepen them? Whether phrased in the enthusiastically scientistic longings of late nineteenth-century positivism or in the metaphysical verbiage of post-Hegelian idealism, philosophers enjoyed successful communication with scientists and theologians, but they couldn't even begin to start a conversation with ordinary folks.

James and Dewey thus found themselves fighting against an entire conception of philosophy: they objected equally to its goals and its methods. A decade after James's death, just after World War I, Dewey began to call for a "reconstruction in philosophy," identifying the Greeks and Descartes as the chief culprits in setting philosophy on the wrong course.

Surprisingly, it is for this rebelliousness that James and Dewey have become heroes to some modern American philosophers. I say "surprisingly" because for a long time pragmatism was taught as if it were just another epistemological and metaphysical system. James and Dewey were studied for their theories of knowledge and truth, not for their revolt against philosophy's basic assumptions. Throughout the twentieth century few philosophers seemed to be aware of the fundamental critique of philosophy that had motivated James and Dewey. Certainly, when the post-Heideggerians tried to deconstruct traditional philosophical assumptions—often much less effectively than the pragmatists—they had no idea that the pragmatists had been there before. Richard Rorty's highly influential *Philosophy and the Mirror of Nature* (1979) created a new trinity of heroes for antiphilosophical philosophers: Dewey, Heidegger, and Wittgenstein.[14] Rorty culled from these new heroes arguments showing that the goal and working assumptions of modern Western philosophy were mistaken.

There is no question that Rorty's book and his subsequent work marked an important transition in late twentieth-century American philosophy. Once again, many philosophers criticized the epistemological assumptions of what Reid had called the ideal theory. Yet Rorty himself—and many of his followers and critics—did not conceive of this criticism as offering a resuscitation of primary experience. In many respects these antitraditionalist philosophers accept much of the traditional subversion of experience: ordinary experience, they are convinced, is unlikely to offer a basis for finding truth or wisdom. They endorse instead a new kind of elitist separation from homely concerns. Rather than align himself with everyday considerations and realities, Rorty continues to extol the activities of Western philosophy, insisting only that philosophers abandon what he sees as their pretensions to having access to deeper truths than anyone else—that is, Rorty recommends that philosophers abandon precisely what they have always claimed made their thinking special.

Hilary Putnam, in his 1994 Dewey lectures, sees this painful situation in philosophy with acute clarity. Unlike Rorty, he has responded not by undermining philosophy as such but by trying to develop a philosophical position that escapes the traps set for it by the Western anti-experiential tradition. Putnam seeks a philosophy that makes contact with primary experience. For Putnam, in contrast to Rorty, the message from James and Dewey is not to abandon philosophy but to reconstruct it. Putnam proposes that we take the first step suggested long ago by Reid—abandon the ideal theory. As Putnam notes, the ideal theory "makes it impossible to see how persons can be in genuine cognitive contact with the world."[15] Furthermore, Putnam urges us to abandon the notion of "ideas in the mind," without severing our ties to natural science. If we could do so, we could achieve a truly major breakthrough: a philosophy that combines the widely acknowledged critique of Cartesianism with the beginnings of a naturalistic alternative philosophical position.

Putnam begins by asking why the realism of the external world has been such a problem for philosophy. Following the arguments of John McDowell, another convert to Reid's basic insight, Putnam explains that "the key assumption responsible for the disaster is that there has to be an interface between our cognitive powers and the external world—or, to put the same point differently, the idea that our cognitive powers cannot reach all the way to the objects themselves."[16] This is a consequence of the scientific revolutionaries' assumption that primary experience "really" is made up of atoms of subjective sensation. If experience is a set of atomic sensations, then to gain useful knowledge of the world around us, we must build up a picture of the world—a representation—using these elements, just as Seurat built up a picture with dots of pigment. The pointillists thus tried to transfer onto canvas what contemporary scientists claimed was "really" going on in our minds, albeit unconsciously, as we saw the world.

This assumption of the need for a cognitive interface (what John Locke in his plain style called ideas) derives from modern philosophy's association with Western science. The primary reason theorists have insisted on cognitive interfaces is their widespread belief in what they call the causal theory of perception. This so-called theory is really more a set of overarching assumptions than a theory—assumptions that have constricted virtually all other theories of perception, philosophical or scientific. The philosophers' main assumption is that, in a scientifically respectable theory of perception, human observers should be considered inert entities—like rocks or billiard balls. Galileo, Descartes, and Etienne de Condillac likened the observer to a statue. And, as usual, what is surprising about this idea of what constitutes a model for perception (a statue as a model of an observer? snapshot vision as a model of looking at things?) is that for the most part philosophers have not commented on the inappropriateness of the conceit. Strange but true: in three centuries and more of theorizing about perception, the notion of studying the active (non-statuelike) processes of looking, listening, and feeling has never been taken up seriously. Philosophers have been content to believe that we experiencers are akin to statues, passively receiving impressions of the world. One of the most important consequences of Gibson's ecological approach to perception was an emphasis on the need to study these activities of information detections.

The idea central to the causal theory of perception is that perception proceeds in two stages. First, a physical stimulus, such as a ray of light, causes a change in the observer (statue). In the second stage, something internal to the observer detects the change and on the basis of this information infers what caused it. According to the theory, what is experienced in this second stage—our sensations—is all that can ever be experienced directly. (Note how everyday primary experience is thus changed into secondhand experience, an inference, like interpreting telegraph messages.) This theory of perception recurs throughout modern philosophy and psychology in a confusing array of variants. Alternative theories are rarely put forward, primarily because they are automatically criticized as naive realism and dismissed out of hand.

Putnam tries to offer an alternative. In an effort to forestall the usual attacks, he announces that he expects to be criticized for his views ("To [many] philosophers what I am calling for will seem to be a re-infantilization of philosophy"). He suggests that his new approach be named "natural realism" because he hopes that it will prove consistent with both everyday experience and scientific knowledge and that it will help us to understand in what sense perception can be said to be true. "The natural realist," Putnam writes, "holds that successful perception is just a seeing, or hearing, or feeling, etc., of things out there; and not a mere affectation of a person's subjectivity by those things." If Putnam is right, philosophers will have to stop beginning courses with "the problem of our knowledge of the external world" because this will no longer be a problem.[17]

The causal theory represents a trap for philosophers because there is no way out once the mind is shut inside the head. Putnam dismisses most theories of how the mind refers to the world as mere "metaphysical magic." At one point he derisively recants his own earlier position by claiming that he imagined something akin to "noetic rays" stretching from the outside into our heads. As Putnam puts it, no causal theorist has come up with an account that avoids making it seem "magical that we can have access to anything outside our 'inputs.' "[18]

It is precisely here that Putnam moves beyond Reid or even Kant. Both earlier philosophers knew that the causal theory made knowledge of the external world problematic. But Reid was willing to accept the magical assertion that God somehow—although Reid admitted not having any idea how—arranged for us to perceive whatever objects caused our sensory impressions. Kant avoided direct reference to God, but few philosophers will think that his appeal to "the transcendental unity of apperception" is anything other than metaphysical magic.

At this juncture, in trying to get away from the causal theory of perception Putnam becomes stuck in a place already scouted out by Bertrand Russell in his *Analysis of Matter* (1927).

Russell argued that the modern philosopher has a fundamental problem: if physics is correct in describing a world made up of matter and motion, then our primary experience cannot be true, for we experience a world rich in meaning, not just a buzzing of atoms. Yet isn't physics in some sense based on our experience? The distance between our physical theories and our experienced world puts the philosopher in a fix. Putnam may have a way out of the jam. He wonders how the idea that nature must be described in physico-mathematical terms came to be "coercive" in philosophy, even though it undermines the meaning and usefulness of ordinary experience. Couldn't physics be true in a way that would not so radically undermine our ordinary view of the world?[19]

The steps Putnam takes to get out of the mess created by the causal theory of perception are tentative. Nevertheless, they appear to be moves in the right direction. Bolstered by James's radical empiricism and some of the careful argumentation in J. L. A. Austin's *Sense and Sensibilia* (1962), Putnam offers three counterarguments to confront the claims typically made in defense of the causal theory.[20]

The first, and weakest, concerns hallucinations and dreams. These abnormal mental states are frequently invoked to "prove" the existence of "cognitive interfaces" or "ideas" in the mind. Surely, when I hallucinate or dream of a dragon I am not seeing a dragon. Yet, equally surely, I am aware of *something* in these cases. Isn't this evidence for the existence of sense data, mental representations—call them what you will? That is, isn't the fact that I am aware of something, when clearly I am perceiving nothing, evidence that what I am aware of in these cases is akin to an internal idea or representation of the world?

The mere assertion that a hallucination involves "sense data," Putnam counters, does not explain these odd mental phenomena. Perhaps not, but all the causal theorist is looking for here is evidence that such sense data exist. It would be nice to have an explanation of hallucinations, but the causal theorist does not need it. The causal theorist can accept Putnam's argument and continue undeterred to disbelieve in direct perception.

A stronger counterargument ought to be given, however. To the extent that causal theory treats perception and hallucination as identical, as simply the having of sense data or mental representations, it undermines the *distinction* between perception and hallucination. (Indeed, there are theorists who seem to want to equate perception with hallucination.) A theory that can help clarify this distinction would therefore be an improvement over causal theory.[21]

Putnam's second argument against causal theorists has to do with their fast-and-loose use of the unconscious. He notes that people with certain pathologies, such as "blindsight," apparently have no visual sense data: these patients vehemently deny being able to see, even though it can be demonstrated that they do see. Such cases force us either to invent a class of "unconscious sense data" (which sounds like a contradiction in terms) or to give up one of the basic claims of the causal theory of perception—that sense data (the data for the second stage in the theory) are immediately and accurately perceived. We do not need to enter the realm of pathology to find such anomalies, however. Consider binocular vision, something common to most human beings. I dare say few readers of this book have ever noticed the doubled images that lie in their visual fields at regions outside the narrow area on which both eyes focus. If after reading this you take the trouble to notice these doublings, have you just brought them into existence, or were they already there? Either way, it is increasingly clear that in many cases—and not just so-called pathological ones—sense data are *not* immediately and accurately perceived.[22]

Finally, Putnam's claims that the identity theory of mind and body on which so much of the causal theory of perception relies is not viable. The identity theory holds that particular neural states can be identified with particular subjective states (in this case, particular sense data). But, as Putnam points out, to accomplish such a theoretical mapping requires a well-articulated theory of the entities involved. And yet "it is not clear that there is a theory of sense data" in this sense. As a philosopher, Putnam appears to be unaware that many psychologists who were contemporary with James tried, in fact, to develop such theories, which would account for all the different kinds of sensory data—and failed. Their idea was to list all the species of color or taste or smell and to develop a complete, non-overlapping set of these species. Not even the genius of Wilhelm Wundt, E. B. Titchener, or G. E. Müller could come up with a consistent and coherent set of sense data for a single sense.

Not long after, it was discovered that both sensory and perceptual states change merely with repeated experience. If you stare at a patch of intense red your sensation of the color red will tend to become "washed out"; if you then look away to a white surface, there will appear a spot with a greenish tinge. (Green is the opposite color to red.) Analogously, simply staring at a curved line (like an open-parenthesis mark) will result in the line's appearing to straighten out and, after you look away, vertical lines in your field of view will appear to be curved in the opposite direction (like a close-parenthesis mark). These results disprove the idea that a sense datum can be identified with a particular stimulus causing a particular change in the observer, and they frustrate the goal of formulating an inventory of sensory data that can be available for interpretation or association with other data. The identity theory of mind-brain sounds good, but when one tries to work out the details, it proves to be impossible.[23] The mental atoms of the scientific revolutionaries turn out to be both changeable and difficult for observers to access—which makes them unsuitable for the job assigned to them.

By thus strengthening his critiques of traditional theories of observation, we can extend Putnam's natural realism. We do not need a new metaphysics to explain how we know the external world; rather, we need to get rid of those ubiquitous Western metaphysical assumptions that force us to question the reality of our experience in this way. As Putnam notes: "Winnowing through to natural realism is seeing the needlessness and unintelligibility of a picture that imposes an interface between ourselves and the world."[24] But philosophers, like nature, abhor a vacuum. Without a theory of experience to replace the causal theory, I doubt that Putnam or his followers will be able to maintain a healthy natural realism. As Putnam himself notes, James and the New Realists came almost as far as he, but lacking an alternative theory of experience, they were unable to persuade philosophers to abandon their old dualistic dogmas.

Putnam needs to do more than assert that his natural realism is consistent with natural science; he needs to offer a theory of perception that is explicitly anti-causal but still scientific. Without this, the old Western philosophical anti-experiential reflexes will knock Putnam's natural realism out of the ring. Luckily, as the examples I have used to amplify his argument suggest, such a perceptual theory has already been developed with a great deal of success by the psychologist James Gibson and his students.

Gibson's ecological approach to perception, as he calls it, makes a radical break with the Western tradition's dismissal of experience. For Gibson, perception is not caused by the world but pursued actively and achieved by the observer. Each observer tries to make sense of his or her surroundings by hunting for meaningful information. Hence, all forms of mental atoms—sensations, ideas, subjective states—are, for the most part, incidental or even useless parts of the perceptual process. The useful aspects of the perceptual process are the stream of activities—looking, listening, feeling, scrutinizing, checking—that yield meaningful information and shapes our experience of a world full of significances, both valuable and dangerous.

But to understand how new and profoundly different Gibson's theory is, we need a deeper appreciation of the connection between anti-experientialism and the goals of Western philosophy. We need to see how and why Western philosophy has turned away from the idea of a meaningful everyday world. We can do this by going back past Putnam to the philosopher in whose honor Putnam offered his natural realism, John Dewey.[25]

# TWO  The Search for a Philosophy of Experience

The close of the twentieth century has brought on a deluge of near-apocalyptic rhetoric from intellectuals. Deconstruction and various other postmodern stances offer an assortment of metaphors of fragmentation, disconnection, and intellectual anomie. Theory and analysis are increasingly abandoned, replaced by verbal shards—some of precious beauty, others pointed and sharp.

In all probability, this situation reflects the "massification" of intellectual culture that has been developing since the 1960s: a large number of highly trained intellectual and cultural workers, increasingly international in their identifications, now constitute a group of their own. One byproduct of this development—and I stress that it is only one—is a tendency to justify one's work solely with reference to a particular in-group and to abandon attempts to speak to those who are outside the charmed circle of intellectuals.

Interestingly, this image of two spheres (a small, cozy, private group of thinkers-in-common separated from the larger circle of society) figures prominently in what Richard Rorty, in

*Contingency, Irony, and Solidarity* (1989), offers as the picture of a "liberal utopia."[1] In his utopia each of us inhabits a rich, autonomous, private sphere. This is the realm in which we create ourselves as we see fit, along with any self-chosen partners we may have. It is essentially a realm in which "anything goes" precisely because it is private and autonomous, a grouping of like-minded individuals. For Rorty each of these many private spheres exists within the larger, "democratic" society as a whole, which, at least in this ideal world, serves the sole function of preventing cruelty (cruelty being one of the possible by-products of the anything-goes kind of self-making in those autonomous spheres).

Rorty's utopia thus resembles the life of intellectuals in modern urban centers and at major universities. In many of these places intellectuals are increasingly sealed off from the everyday concerns of most people. With extraordinary job security, considerable control over work rules and work time, and extensive access to travel and media, these intellectual workers are far less constrained by the "belt-tightening" processes that have been felt by workers in other fields, or even, for that matter, by teachers in less prestigious institutions, such as state colleges and high schools. Although academics could use their intellectual skills to help solve real problems, nowadays they rarely create genuine links between intellectual work and problems outside the academy.

Thus there is a tendency for philosophers and theorists to become separated from all everyday experience except . . . intellectual experience. Perhaps it is no wonder that these thinkers increasingly dismiss the construction of cogent, empirically based, explanatory theories as passé. Many in the academic world have latched onto such recent developments as deconstruction because they see it as liberating to abandon even the attempt to build coherent, empirical accounts of the real world. What succeeds best in the new intellectual world is not so much the true or the useful as the clever and the fashionable—what used to dominate the conversations of salons now fills our books. There is, after all, little motivation to distinguish between the cognitive and the aesthetic value of an intellectual work when there is no practical realm within which to assess that cognitive value— besides, what matters to most intellectuals is how other intellectuals react to and appropriate their work.

In such a world, drained of real experience, it is also not surprising that philosophical theorizing begins to take on the aura of fable. After all, people lacking in experience are childlike in many ways, and fables are appropriate to a childlike mentality. Consider Rorty's utopia and his ethical theory, which he self-consciously sums up in phrases like "cause no harm" and "don't be cruel." In this utopia, Rorty prides himself on having solved the problem of relativism by endorsing the notion of many relatively independent communities, each with its own standards and rules—all constrained by the simple general injunction to avoid cruelty. Such a theory is fablelike in its schematic nature and oversimplicity. Like folktales of many sorts and children's favorites from the Brothers Grimm through Dr. Seuss, it takes no effort in Rorty's tale to discriminate the good from the evil characters. This is a particularly distressing feature of an ethical theory in the twentieth century, a period in which the most heinous crimes have been couched in the language and gesture of doing good, and at a time when many of us are genuinely concerned about how difficult it can be to distinguish good from evil.

In fact, Rorty's injunctions are little more than the stock lessons of children's literature. One could find countless examples, but I give one from *Black Beauty*, a favorite of my daughter's. One of the boys in the stable relates a lesson learned from his teacher: "He talked to all the boys very seriously about cruelty, and said how hard-hearted and cowardly it was to hurt the weak and the helpless; but what stuck in my mind was this: he said that cruelty was the devil's own trademark, and if we saw anyone who took pleasure in cruelty we might know who he belonged to."[2]

These are sensible words, and Rorty's attacks on cruelty are sensible and well-intentioned. Rorty even notes that he is trying to secularize moral messages that have traditionally been couched in theological language, which is what is done in classic children's literature (like *Black Beauty* or the books of Frances Hodgson Burnett). The problem with Rorty (or with these children's books, for that matter) is not what he does but what he fails to do: this message against cruelty is important, but it doesn't go very far. Most people know and accept Rorty's lesson; many remember the injunction not to do harm even as they are harming others. Much more needs to be done and said if we are to develop a moral and political theory suitable for adults, especially now, when our standards for treating other human beings have reached such appalling lows.[3]

Rorty seems to agree that the mere evasion of cruelty is not enough—but he argues that any theory that tries to establish a general good beyond the avoidance of cruelty is inevitably *coercive*. "What counts as being a decent human being is relative to historical circumstance, a matter of transient consensus about what attitudes are normal and what practices are just or unjust."[4] This, sadly, is indeed a historical fact. The behavior of most of us urbanites in the 1990s toward the homeless, for example, would have been widely chastised as indecent a mere thirty years ago. Yet Rorty uses this historical truth to promote a conceptual falsehood—the claim that we *cannot* offer sound general arguments for how people should treat one another. He argues that this is because what we call knowledge is nothing more than a disguised form of utility—itself a disguised form of power. Hence, when philosophers (or others) urge us toward a particular moral stand on the basis of a knowledge of human nature or of what is good for human beings, they are in fact engaging in a form of coercion.

Rorty's good intentions are thus hobbled by, of all things, his allegiance to part of the philosophical tradition he claims to be overcoming—the idea that experience is all in the mind. He *assumes* that experience cannot inform us about values and significance. He assumes that what people experience as cruel (or as good) is really a judgment, an inference, based on subjective sense data. And because these subjective data are not meaningful in themselves, he thinks that someone else might interpret them differently. Now it is of course true that different people often interpret a situation in different ways—but this does not mean that they do so because they are interpreting their sense data differently! They may perceive the situation as meaningful but differ in their construal of the meaning. When an American teenager was arrested in Singapore and caned for committing a misdemeanor, most Americans understood that the caning was a way of punishing someone via public humiliation—the argument was over whether this kind of humiliation was appropriate. Rorty—and many other thinkers—act as if we do not concur on the meanings of such cases, and I suggest that this is, simply, false.

If Rorty is right, we should abandon the search for the common good. Indeed, if he is right we should realize that what we thought was a search for the common good was nothing of the sort, but was instead an attempt to impose our values on other people, who presumably held legitimate views of their own. Because, if Rorty is right, we would have to impose our values on others for them to be able to see a situation as meaning what we see it as meaning. This is why Rorty argues for the "end of philosophy" as we know it. If the question "How shall I live?" cannot be answered in any general sense; if it can be answered only in the same way we answer "What sort of foods suit my taste?"; then surely what we have come to think of as philosophy is dead—and good riddance.

Luckily, the question "How shall I live?" does not really have the same sort of answers as a question about what tickles my taste buds. We can give real, helpful answers to this question, and we can even evaluate the answers. The ability to do this, however, can only come from a philosophy that is as engaged with the world of primary experience as Rorty and others like him are disengaged. The truth is that Rorty's theory is in this regard no different from the tradition he claims to reject: Rorty is unwilling to grant meaning to primary experience, and he seems determined to keep everyday concerns at a distance from his serious philosophy.

In contrast to Rorty, one of his heroes, the exemplary, engaged philosopher John Dewey, saw primary experience as the root of all meaning and rejected the Cartesian theory of perception. All Dewey's philosophy—from his epistemology and ontology to his social theory—assumes a world in which people share meanings, however much they disagree about how to use those meanings. Dewey's philosophy was largely directed toward showing how, given this sharing of meaning, progress could be made toward answering questions about the way we should live.[5]

### DEWEY'S PHILOSOPHY OF FREEDOM

Reading Dewey's critiques of the Western philosophical tradition nowadays, in the midst of arguments over canonformation and multiculturalism, one feels an uncanny sense of recognition. In such books as *Reconstruction in Philosophy,* written in 1919, Dewey seems to have anticipated a great deal of the current debate. He attacks the Western tradition not just for having bad ideas but for buttressing an oppressive social order. In what other philosopher of Dewey's day could one read a critique of Plato and Aristotle that emphasized that they were active participants in a slave society?[6]

Dewey criticized traditional Western philosophy's "quest for certainty" and its obsession with finding unchanging essences, not just because these ideas are bad philosophy but because they are also elitist and anti-democratic. For Dewey, a concern with unchanging essences reflects an unhealthy separation of knower from doer, of an intellectual, elitist ruling class from ordinary working stiffs.

For many nowadays, Dewey's recognition that the quest for *certainty* is elitist as well as untenable has been turned into the belief that the quest for *knowledge* is elitist and untenable. Rorty, for example, will only defend the quest for knowledge when it is a private activity within one of his autonomous spheres, and he explicitly denies that a universal encouragement to search for knowledge should be endorsed. But Dewey never rejected the quest for knowledge—he simply rejected its elitist incarnations throughout the history of Western thought.

In fact, Dewey's goal might be summarized as the democratization of philosophy and of the quest for knowledge. This was to be accomplished through a democratization of experience, supported by such institutions as schools and workplaces and also by political institutions. Such a broad-based collectivizing of experience—remember, in Dewey's terms experience is the process, not its products—was for Dewey the new basis of philosophy. "How shall *I* live?" as a guiding question is gradually replaced by "How shall *we* live?": a question genuinely addressed to everyone but for each of us to answer in our own way. Moreover, as I shall show below, Dewey's conception of shared experience was not a child's fable of good guys and bad guys but a mature realization of the complexities of people and circumstances.

The first stage in Dewey's argument is the realization that what he calls negative freedom is not enough. Dewey defines negative freedom as freedom from constraint: in the realm of ideas it is freedom from censorship; in the realm of action, it is freedom from inhibitions, internal or external. Negative freedoms are what civil libertarians (like Dewey) defend passionately and what Rorty has enshrined in the autonomous zones of his liberal utopia.[7]

Negative freedom is a limited kind of freedom. As Dewey insisted, in order to enjoy negative freedom a person already has to *be a person,* with wants, needs, and interests. But for a person to become a person—for these wants, needs, and inter-

cording to each person's lights. Yet most modern philosophers would read this alternative as nothing more than a variant of "anything goes." Without a universalized, essentialist touchstone against which to measure different experiences and attitudes, they would claim that Dewey's goal of personal growth is simply a license for any and every form of behavior imaginable. If it were defined in this way, personal growth would not be able to figure in the reconstruction of philosophy.

But Dewey does not embrace relativism of the anything-goes variety precisely because his emphasis on self-growth is not an attempt to seek a universal truth. As Putnam pointed out, Dewey adamantly rejected the idea that there is, could be, or should be one, absolute conception of the world. "Dewey held that the idea of a single theory that explains everything has been a disaster in the history of philosophy."[9] Dewey insisted that we should abandon this pernicious dream and strive to make philosophy an activity that helps us to resolve real problems as they emerge in daily life, "local problems," if one wants to call them that. For Dewey, the solving of such local problems constitutes self-realization. To those obsessed with solutions to general philosophical problems, this may sound overly modest; however, I remind the reader that among the local problems of burning importance in many parts of our world as this is written are such matters as how different ethnic groups can learn to live together in peace—hardly an issue one would want to trivialize with the somewhat misleading label of local problem.

When Dewey writes that "freedom is found in that kind of interaction which maintains an environment in which human desire and choice count for something," he is not stating a universal truth but making a pragmatic suggestion.[10] To help people become who they want to be we need a supportive environment. This is true even when there is no single definition of a supportive environment. After all, you might best learn how to swim if I throw you into deep water; whereas I might best learn how to

ests to germinate (much less flower)—one needs positive conditions, not just negative freedom. Dewey speaks of those who emphasize only negative freedom as being engaged in "a romantic glorification of natural impulse as something superior to all moral claims." Such unrestrained creativity is often supposed to be a form of self-discovery, but this view incorrectly identifies what is *least* individually distinctive with self-realization. As Dewey put it: "Although appetites are the commonest things i human nature, the least distinctive or individualized" psycholo ical processes, proponents of negative freedom falsely iden "unrestraint in satisfaction of appetite with free realizatior individuality."[8]

What Dewey has in mind here is a homely point, u stood by thoughtful parents. To take an obvious example children have a remarkably robust appetite for watching sion. Should we say, as the theory of negative freedom s that an unrestrained opportunity to indulge in televisior ing is a free realization of our children's individuality Such unrestrained opportunity for indulgence is ofte posite of free development. The child whom we he how to choose what to do and when to do it is the becomes most capable of developing her individua child who knows only how to satisfy her cravings. are competent at satisfying their cravings. We are vidual when we indulge our appetites; we become ourselves when we learn how to exercise choice a

What *is* the free realization of individu negative freedom? This is the question behind m Dewey's philosophy. If we cannot give a mean able alternative here, then we should get rid discipline and replace it with private discussion

Dewey thought he did have an alter freedom as lack of constraint: freedom as gen as the growth and enrichment of each per

swim only by sticking my toes in first and taking one small step at a time. Dewey's philosophy does not require that a universally helpful formula be found beyond this one: that for humans to flourish in any given instance they must have the kind of support they need. This is by no means as empty a statement as it might at first sound. For one thing, it forces us to deal with the *irrevocably collective* element in human flourishing and experience. For us to make flourishing possible requires collective effort and interaction among many people. Individual human freedom cannot be separated from collective freedom. And, Dewey argued, human knowledge and experience are not the possessions of individuals but of groups, which should (but do not always) promote the growth of all their members.

### HUMAN NATURE AND ITS MIRRORS

Rorty and other postmodern thinkers insist that the Enlightenment ideal of human solidarity—of motivating action solely on the basis of shared humanity—is dead. In contrast, as we have seen, Dewey believes in binding individual human freedom to collective freedom. Dewey holds that human growth (what he calls human flourishing) necessarily refers to people in groups, not to individuals.[11]

This contrast between Dewey and the postmodern thinkers is striking, because the basis most often cited for the rejection of the Enlightenment ideal of human solidarity—that philosophical theory cannot mirror reality—is one with which Dewey agrees. Rorty and others have rightly attacked the idea of philosophical theory as a "mirror" of reality, whether it be a mirror of the external world or of human nature. They wish to replace classical Western philosophy's emphasis on "representation" (as in, "the mind accurately represents reality") with an emphasis on habit or activity (as in, "this is what we *do*"). Nothing could sound more Deweyan—in almost all Dewey's writings on this subject he argues against the idea of a fixed logic or rationality or representation and for the notion of activity-based modes of inquiry.[12]

But the similarity between Dewey and critics of the Enlightenment ideal begins and ends with this rejection of the conception of philosophy as a mirror of nature. Dewey's conception of activity or habit is much richer than that of Rorty or the postmodernists in general. Dewey did not accept the traditional idea that our minds mirror or represent the world; nevertheless, he still tried to understand how our activities show cognizance of the world, how what we do is meaningful and makes sense. Many anti-Enlightenment thinkers, such as Rorty, eschew any belief in meanings that transcend local groups of interpreters. Rorty, for example, explicitly equates speech with the mere making of noises, arguing that the meanings all come from our interpretation of these noises.[13] Apparently, for all his rejection of the philosophical tradition, Rorty still considers the primary experience of speaking to be the mere making of noises, which the listener must interpret and give meaning to by means of refined subjective processes.

For Dewey, on the contrary, primary experience is already meaningful; for Dewey, even habit is meaningful and subject to growth. Habit and activity for him are not purely physiological happenings but are instead meaningful ways of changing one's environment. Fundamentally, we experience the world in terms of what it means for us; even our habits are geared toward discovering these meanings—habits are not merely mechanical and reflexive. For Dewey a habit is not chewing your fingernails; it is a birdwatcher's knowing where to look for interesting birds. If free self-development is the basic good, then what makes an action or a habit good is its openness to growth and development. (Note that nothing has yet been said about the goal of development—I am still talking about people making themselves according to their own lights.)

Thus, Dewey writes: "What makes a habit bad is enslavement to old ruts. The common notion that enslavement to good ends converts mechanical routine into good is a negation of the principles of moral goodness. It identifies morality with what *was* [once] rational [but is so no more]. . . . The genuine heart of reasonableness (and of goodness in conduct) lies in effective mastery of the conditions which *now* enter into action." Unlike mental representation or mirrors, actions do not reflect the world. The representational metaphor so fundamental to centuries of Western thought is a misleading one, as Rorty teaches us. Yet although actions do not represent or mirror the world, they can be more or less in tune with the environment, and actors can be more or less aware of their surroundings, as Dewey teaches us. Thus, the fundamental human virtue for Dewey becomes what he, perhaps unfortunately, called docility—defined as the eagerness "to learn all the lessons of active, inquiring, expanding experience." Again, Dewey is not postulating a particular kind of experience or content of experience as "the good." He is focusing on experience as a process, as part of human activity in the environment.[14]

The critique of Rorty's utopia and of similar anti-Enlightenment theorizing that I can offer on this basis is straightforward. As a human being, my own growth cannot be isolated from the activities, experiences, and growth of other people. On the contrary, my growth is intricately and immensely indebted to collective experience, collectively obtained resources, and complex networks of interaction. This seems obvious in the 1990s, when the food we eat, the clothes we wear, and the songs we whistle come from far and wide, and when every aspect of our lives is deeply intertwined with the activities of countless other people. Perhaps postmodern, anti-Enlightenment theorists fail to see this fundamentally collective nature of experience because nowadays we do not meet enough people to experience them for ourselves and interact with them in meaningful ways. We live in a world of interdependent communication and economic *systems* that have substituted for the interdependence of human *beings*. The potential richness and vitality of human interdependence have been seriously compromised by our modern institutions of work, school, and communication, which have tended to constrain the growth of interaction and community. I shall discuss these issues further in Chapters 3 and 4.

There is no need to theorize the existence of an essential "human nature" underlying our actions and attitudes to justify the ideal of supporting experience and its growth. It is enough to try to understand our own selves and their potential for growth. Philosophers, Dewey argued, should not worry about the problem of "How can I know *überhaupt* [overall and completely]? but How shall I think *here and now*? Not what is a test of thought at large, but what validates and confirms *this* thought?"[15] Here and now what we really do not need are more excuses to curl up in our own intellectual cocoons. For one thing, life outside those cocoons is getting so grim that soon there will no longer be sufficient support in the environment for intellectual caterpillars or butterflies.

For action to be conducive to freedom in Dewey's sense it cannot be separated from either the environment or other people. Only through action do we transform our environment, and freedom can be promoted only by making the environment more supportive of docility—of human flourishing. To coordinate the actions of many people for a single goal requires *collective action* or, in other words, it requires *social institutions*.

Dewey's philosophy is inseparable from his sociology and social psychology for just this reason. Philosophizing does not concern only abstractions of mind or nature; it deals with real problems faced by real people trying to become free, in Dewey's sense. Hence, the philosophy of freedom must at least in part be about the building and preserving of freedom-promoting institutions.[16] Yet, sadly, not only the late twentieth-century philosophers but our populace on the whole have become convinced that institutions are the *opponents* of freedom. Dewey strongly condemned such thinking, in a passage worth quoting at length:

> To view institutions as enemies of freedom, and all conventions as slaveries, is to deny the only means by which positive freedom in action can be secured. A general liberation of impulses may set things going when they have been stagnant, but if the released forces are on their way to anything they do not know the way nor where they are going. Indeed, they are bound to be mutually contradictory and hence destructive—destructive not only of the habits they wish to destroy, but of themselves, of their own efficacy. Convention and custom are necessary to carrying forward impulse to any happy conclusion. A romantic return to nature and a freedom sought within the individual without regard to the existing environment finds its terminus in chaos. Every belief to the contrary combines pessimism regarding the actual with an even more optimistic faith in some natural harmony or other—a faith which is a survival of some of the traditional metaphysics and theologies which professedly are to be swept away. Not convention but stupid and rigid convention is the foe. And, as we have noted, a convention can be reorganized and made mobile only by using some other custom for giving leverage to an impulse.[17]

The individualism that is so deeply rooted in our thought, our culture, and our actions is probably the biggest obstacle to our development of a genuine philosophy of freedom and experience, and it certainly is the biggest obstacle to our development of a genuine social practice of freedom. This individualism cannot be uprooted by mere thought or mere words, as Dewey well knew. To overcome such a powerful cultural assumption will take concerted and diligent action. What philosophy and other intellectual pursuits can offer are not easy solutions—no universal truths—but reasonable suggestions for guidance and reasonable encouragement to further our own growth. "A false psychology of an isolated self and a subjective morality shuts out from morals the things important to it, acts and habits in their objective consequences."[18] Thus, to open ourselves and our moral theories up to what is important to them requires looking at acts and their consequences in context. Dewey not only knew this but he acted upon it from fairly early in his career, becoming a student of education, of work, and of social life.

The analysis of the problems of life in everyday settings—like schools or workplaces—was, for Dewey, a part of philosophy. In spite of our postmodern sophistication, few modern intellectuals can claim to have given significant thought to these contexts. Philosophers—especially postmodern ones—need to spend more of their time thinking about the places within which people find themselves (schools, workplaces, in front of the television) and less time dealing with abstractions. It is indicative of the trend of much of modern science that the study of human thinking—cognitive science, as it has come to be called—is best exemplified by studies of how people think when forced to respond rapidly to a display on a video monitor. Currently, the cutting edge in cognitive science involves strapping subjects into a PETscan or similar device (a machine for reading and mapping brain activity) and giving them simple makework problems, such as mental arithmetic. But one cannot *do* much of anything when strapped into these scanning machines. Thus, through the magic of information technology, studying how people think when they are not doing anything becomes elevated into "cognitive neuroscience."

Dewey, of course, did not seal himself off. His criticism of the educational system is well known, albeit by name only. But how many who think they know what "Deweyan education" means realize that the goal of Dewey's proposed reforms was to democratize the experience of children at schools, in order to decrease imitation (slavish habits) and increase thoughtful action (good habits and docility)? And I suspect that fewer still know that Dewey offered a powerful critique of the modern workplace for making mechanical rut the ruler of our lives for so many hours of the day.[19] Freedom, like experience, is a process. The conditions for furthering it are collective and institutional, not personal or private. Many of us modern intellectuals pride ourselves on our "liberal" views and stand against those who oppose civil liberties, those who intend to negate the negative freedoms so dearly won by modern societies. But however valuable this defense of negative freedoms is, it cannot offer a complete or adequate defense of freedom. Those whose actions—or inactions—weaken the institutions on which all human growth (not just their own) depend are also enemies of freedom. The loss of widespread access to effective schooling or meaningful work—a loss that is no longer the bad dream of a few pessimists but a real prospect for many people—will be just as damaging to our freedoms as the passing of, say, censorship laws. The disarray among intellectuals over the benefits embodied in schooling and work, and the lack of an explicit movement to promote the democratization of experience, is one of the saddest features of our times.

### PROSPECTS FOR PROGRESS

Dewey agrees with the anti-Enlightenment thinkers that universal philosophical questions are bogus. We have no need to know either truth or reality as such. And, in all likelihood, we do not even know what these labels signify. But rejecting such views of philosophy is not the same as rejecting philosophy. Dewey, as a philosopher, asked a fundamental question, which we would do well to ponder. What are the conditions for human growth in our society? How can we promote that growth widely enough to address, as a society, this question democratically, from diverse viewpoints? Do schools encourage the kind of growth in experience that would help in collectivizing our quest? Do workplaces? If these institutions do not promote human growth, what can we do to help them move toward that goal?

The conception of human growth used here is not intended to be a new absolute, some ideal entity outside of history against which our everyday life can be measured. Yet neither is this concept of human growth a circumscribed, culturally bound prejudice. It is a judgment—a philosophical judgment—about *our* reality and where *we* stand. It is not apodictically certain: it is what I think can be reasonably said to describe our situation. And it is eminently revisable. When subjected to serious criticism it will undoubtedly need to be revised, yet revision will not undermine its present value. If it turns out, for example, that my neo-Deweyan approach to education fails to accomplish the goals I have set for it and needs to be replaced by a different approach, will we not at least have learned something useful about the important issue of what is an effective style of teaching? The fundamental value endorsed here, the idea that promoting human growth should be a basic goal of work and school is, in other words, a universal philosophical claim not of the absolutist sort, but of the sort Dewey envisaged: "Philosophy has always claimed universality for itself. It will make its claim good when it connects this universality with the formation of directive hypotheses instead of with a sweeping pretension to knowledge of Universal Being. That hypotheses are fruitful when they are suggested by actual need, are bulwarked by knowledge already attained, and are tested by the operations they evoke goes without saying."[20]

I am glad Dewey spelled out what goes without saying, because it certainly does not go without saying. Many philosophers are still striving for their holy grail of absolute truth. Their opponents insist that it cannot be found. Yet instead of telling us how things are actually known—hypothetically, subject to revision, but still known—both the absolutists and their opponents have concocted an intellectual fantasy world, a kind of mental playground where nothing is knowable. Postmodernists taunt the heirs of the Enlightenment with the claim that nothing can really be known—a claim they take from the Enlightenment's own deepest philosophers, Hume and Kant. A typical response to this among academic philosophers has been to try to find some absolute truth or reality—something behind or beyond experience. But a more useful response to this kind of relativism, as the anthropologist Clifford Geertz has suggested, is *not* to offer an essentialist or absolutist counterclaim but to reject the debate altogether. Absolutism and relativism are two sides of the same debased intellectual coin—the search for a guaranteed truth. Relativism teaches us that sacred truths can eventually turn out to be wrong. And anti-relativism teaches us that at the heart of all knowledge there is valuable human experience that we can try to share, even if we never fully succeed in doing so.[21]

Our actions change the environment, but they also change us. Experience goes hand in hand with action, and both can be improved and enlarged. One really can learn from one's mistakes. Philosophers and scientists, like the rest of us, must gain their knowledge of things from their own experience or from others who have competence in certain areas. Thus, philosophy has no choice but to accept "the goods that are diffused in human experience. [Philosophy] has no Mosaic or Pauline authority of revelation entrusted to it. But it has the authority of intelligent criticism of these common and natural goods."[22] Dewey should have added that philosophy has the authority of intelligent criticism only to the extent that it will *take* that authority, to the extent that philosophers will *risk being wrong* in the service of our collective human effort to understand and improve ourselves. A fear of uncertainty is pervasive in the modern world, and it has crippled, among other things, many philosophers' attempts to use intelligent criticism in the service of humanity.

Practical action and thought can improve us, even if they cannot perfect us. There is no need for a heroic and specialist expertise that isolates philosophers so that they can achieve certainty—as, unfortunately, has been characteristic of Western philosophy. Instead, we must create situations in which people can work together at enlarging and improving their experience, to create the possibility of intelligent criticism. This will require education that emphasizes personal experience and its growth and conditions of daily life that foster genuine collaboration and cooperation.

Philosophers should not hope to transmit truths to their students, in Dewey's view. Instead, "the best we can accomplish for posterity is to transmit unimpaired and with some increment of meaning the environment that makes it possible to maintain the habits of decent and refined life."[23] Looked at from this perspective, we late twentieth-century citizens and intellectuals are failures. The human environment we are bequeathing to our children and students is increasingly degraded of meaning, not to mention downright dangerous. Indeed, I hope to show that the degradation of experience embodied in the *theories* of the Western tradition has by now become a degradation of experience itself in many aspects of everyday life. Hence, an ecological defense of experience should have practical, as well as theoretical, value.

# THREE    Fear of Uncertainty and the
Flight from Experience

In the late twentieth century we are beginning to lose the ability
to experience our world directly. What we have come to *mean* by
the term *experience* is impoverished; what we *have* of experience
in daily life is impoverished as well. Why is this? I believe that
one reason is that the philosophical attitude toward experience—
which I have shown to be undermining our ability to understand
how experience is meaningful—is (and has been for close to four
hundred years) deeply embedded in the institutions of modern
everyday life. From the computerized telephone sales pitch to the
check-out line at the grocery store, from the typing pool to the
assembly line, our experience is being impoverished and degraded. I suggest that the cause of this degradation is the same in
everyday life as it is in philosophy: the fear of uncertainty.

From the Cartesian philosophers our intellectuals learned
to divide experience into two different, but equally mechanical
processes, effectively eliminating primary experience from our
worldview. As a culture we Americans are in danger of losing sight
of the value of primary experience. Further, modern industrial

processes have so altered production practices that they undermine the hope of working people to gain meaningful experience on the job. And because our theorists have lost sight of the value of primary experience, few have defended either the workers or their need for experience. Just as modern mass-market industrialization has created a world in which most bread is a mildly glutinous substance filled with air and assorted impurities, so these processes have created a world in which experience is a flickering montage beamed to us via satellite. The lack of rich, chewy, crusty bread can be cured not by going back to the old days but by making bread carefully—which requires paying attention, using the right ingredients, and learning from the recipes of good bakers. Inevitably, the bread makers must care as much about making a good product as about the profits from that product. Similarly, the lack of rich, chewy, crusty experience can be cured only by careful attention to the proper ingredients and procedure.

### THE EVIL DEMON

As daily life has become increasingly routine and mechanized, our experience of and encounters with other people tend to diminish. Those of us who commute to work by automobile see others as little more than metal-shelled impediments to our own travel. While walking or taking public transportation, urban commuters become virtual automata, speeding to places of work as if on conveyor belts, attending not to the task at hand or to the view but to their own thoughts. They appear to be mere husks of humanity, presumably alive in their thoughts alone, as their bodies progress automatically through the world. It takes a leap of faith, almost, to see them as animate creatures: "If I look out of the window and see men crossing the square, as I just happen to have done, I normally say that I see the men themselves. . . . Yet do I see any more than hats and coats which could conceal automatons? I *judge* that they are men. And so something which I thought I was seeing with my eyes is in fact grasped solely by the faculty of judgment which is in my mind." Written 350 years ago, Descartes's comment seems to be an eerily appropriate description of the daily round of modern life.[1]

But Descartes's observation was not meant to describe our modern automated way of life; rather, Descartes was making a subtle distinction between two kinds of experience, between sight, which uses the eyes, and a kind of perception that exercises the mind. Should judgment really be thought of as separate from experience? Here is the first step that leads to philosophy's disregard of the everyday and its false analysis of experience. Are there really two different kinds of visual experience, a "basic" kind in which we receive impressions of the shapes and motions of things, and a "more refined," interpretive experience, in which we infer the significance of the things around us? Do we see people's bodies in one way and their minds in another? Is it really the case that I see a person's hat differently from the way I see his boredom or her grim determination to carry out her daily tasks, as Descartes implies? To prove his claim, Descartes would have to demonstrate the difference between the experience of seeing and that of judging what we see. But he doesn't. He does not show, for example, that our subjective experience when we see the color of a hat is different from our subjective experience when we see a bored visage. Instead, he rests his argument on the peculiar supposition that "there is some supremely powerful and . . . malicious deceiver, who is deliberately trying to deceive me in every way he can." This deceitful demon could fill clothes with robots and thus confuse us about what is real and what is not.

If there were such a malicious demon, we would need to find a guaranteed process for acquiring true experience—some sort of machinelike algorithm to save us from human missteps—or we would never know what was happening around us (a conclusion some post-Cartesian philosophers are happy to embrace). Descartes originally envisaged our psychological mechanism as having two parts: a bodily machinery for gathering sensations and a mental machinery for making judgments on the basis of those sensations. While Descartes's suggestion that we have bodily machinery for sensing has been influential for centuries, his proposal that purely mental judgment might also be machinelike has become influential only with the rise of computers and "artificial intelligence" and with the advent of recent theories that equate human mental processes with computers and their programs.

Descartes's "evil demon" is the conspiracy theory to end all conspiracy theories. It allows the philosopher to conceive of a powerful conspiracy designed to make us disbelieve in the reality of this world (the one we have always experienced) when, in "truth" (at least according to the conspiracy theory) a completely different world exists. This is intellectual sleight-of-hand, and yet Descartes achieves his complete undermining of ordinary reality without offering any evidence. All one needs to prove his theory, he suggests, is evidence that the senses are not always reliable.

Philosophers have dubbed this intellectual maneuver "the argument from illusion," and it occupies a central place in most modern discussions of our knowledge of the external world. In its crudest form, this argument states that because we know that our senses sometimes lie, we cannot *ever* accept the evidence of the senses *alone* as real knowledge. Having undermined everyday perception, each philosopher then brings in his own favorite source of truth to replace ordinary experience. Descartes, for example, rejected his sensory experiences as untrustworthy but accepted his pure thought as reliable. Indeed, he claimed that his pure thought had convinced him that the world is not really as we experience it but is instead made up of molecules in motion.

But this is nonsense. No sensible person would equate evidence showing that his or her senses are occasionally unreliable with evidence that the world is nothing like what it seems. The whole purpose of conspiracy theories is to make people think in ways that are not sensible, usually on the basis of one plausible fact, and Descartes's theory succeeds in this admirably. The plausible fact is that our senses are sometimes unreliable—but why should this mean that the world is deceptive and that our primary experience is useless?

Even if we accept Descartes's delusion about an evil demon for the sake of the argument, it does not justify his distinction between a basic visual experience and a more refined experience based on thought and judgment. Descartes did not believe that even the most evil of demons could deceive a person about his or her own state of consciousness: "Let him deceive me as much as he can, he will never bring it about that I am nothing so long as I think that I am something." In short—I think, therefore I am. The evil demon who fools me into thinking that robots are men could also fool me about those hats, but no evil demon could fool me about the fact that I am thinking, or so Descartes held. Descartes thus argued that the second stage in perception—thinking and interpreting—is less subject to error than the process as a whole. Although this is a case of special pleading, many theorists, even today, seem to believe that an individual can always give an account of his own mental state, even when he may be unable to determine other happenings.

If he had followed his idea about the evil demon more consistently, Descartes should have concluded that we never, strictly speaking, experience anything except our own mental states: either all sight is a kind of thought or judgment (and thus has the element of certainty that Descartes believed was provided by pure mental activity), or no sight is certain, and my eyes continually deceive me, even the thinking me. Descartes did not arrive at these conclusions, however, because they would have undermined one of his primary goals: a reevaluation of the nature of daily experience that would help support the very uncommonsensical conclusions of the new "mechanical philosophy" of the scientific revolution. (Indeed, Descartes tried to fudge this whole issue by arguing that some experiential ideas could be vetted by pure thought, and if they proved to be clear and distinct, they could then be accepted as true. I return to this point below.)

In his role as a proponent of the new science, Descartes needed to avoid complete skepticism about the senses because a person who believes in the illusory nature of sense perception is unlikely to be enthusiastic about the prospects for science. On the other hand, someone who believes that we truly *see* such things as another's *feelings* must admit much more in his or her philosophy than is usually allowed into a scientific worldview. With the advent of modern mechanistic science, feelings and many other phenomena were relegated to the realm of unreality—treated as "subjective additions" to a world that was made up solely of particles of matter in motion.[2] Descartes was content to say that the corporeal person had physical existence, that our bodies are made up of matter in motion. But, for Descartes, the feeling and thinking person could not have the same objective status as our bodily selves because feeling and thinking are made out of different stuff altogether, being composed of a mental substance not to be found anywhere in the physical world. Descartes is famed for his mind-body dualism, but he (and other proponents of the scientific revolution) also launched a dualism that separated the active, physical, embodied self from the contemplative, thinking self.[3]

The body became a nonthinking mechanism that allegedly carried out certain processes (for example, respiration) infallibly, thus leaving the mind free to be a judging mechanism for creating what Descartes called clear and distinct ideas on the basis of murky sensations. The everyday experience of most observers, who gradually learn about their world through trial and error and other such messy procedures, is thus left out of the account. For Descartes and for philosophers of the subsequent Western tradition, certainty became associated with the thinking mind and the nonthinking body. Confusion and uncertainty were increasingly associated with the everyday self, which combines mind and body in a decidedly unclear and indistinct manner. No idea has been more pernicious in the Western tradition than the assumption that knowledge equals certainty, which equals a divorce from everyday experience.

### THE MACHINING OF THE MIND

In his fear of uncertainty more than in his science, Descartes truly anticipated the modern world. Descartes not only wanted his scientific results to be certain—like his mathematical proofs—but he dreamed of a world in which all purely mental processes would produce equally solid and certain results. Knowing that experience is often deceptive, Descartes was determined both to reduce our reliance on ordinary experience and to distinguish between two kinds of mental activity during experience. The first kind of mental activity does not produce certainty, for it does not involve higher or pure mental processes—it is what remains of primary experience in Descartes's world, and it tends to be called subjective sensory experience, or something like that. The second kind of mental activity is "pure," yielding certainty because it is based on Descartes's "clear and distinct" ideas. For Descartes, the best example of such pure thought was a mathematical proof.

After Descartes, the scientific study of perception slowly incorporated Descartes's fear of uncertainty into various versions of the two-stage theory of perception. Eventually, the scientific desire for certainty led to the complete undermining of primary experience. We are told that, strictly speaking, we never see any *thing*. What we see, this odd but ubiquitous theory holds, are spots of light and color, which affect our brains—so-called visual sensations or sense data—not things of any sort. We can gain clear and distinct ideas of patches of color, but we are likely to be mistaken about objects. I, for one, have occasionally mistaken a stranger for a friend because I was fooled by her looks—haven't we all? But Cartesians claim that all meaningful sight (that is, the seeing of objects or people) is in reality a combination of the two mechanisms, bodily and mental: sensation plus judgment. In the scientific version of this metaphor, we are brains in a vat, struggling to interpret whatever dregs of transmitted information we might locate. According to Descartes and many subsequent thinkers, our best bet is to identify clear and distinct ideas we already hold and use these to interpret all subsequent inputs. Many twentieth-century theories of knowledge have held that knowledge involves taking one's subjective states and trying to test whether they fit current or upcoming realities.

Just how debilitating the Cartesian view of experience is can best be shown by example. When we meet a person and wish to know whether he is deceiving us (being dishonest with regard to some joint enterprise, for example), how, according to Descartes, should we go about finding out? The commonsense method—just observe him closely—is ruled out. The problem with following this pragmatic, basic, commonplace method, for Descartes, is that the judgment might be wrong (which of course it might be). According to Descartes, we should rather evaluate the person in terms of all our knowledge—about *anything*—and then connect our current observations of him with this prior knowledge. Thus, if we firmly believe that certain groups of people are always dishonest, we should start our evaluation with this preconceived idea, not with careful scrutiny of the individual. The idea here is to creep along, starting from known (clear and distinct) truths, not from our experience of the person in question. The resemblance of Descartes's method to paranoia is striking and disturbing: I "know" you Jews (Russians, homosexuals—fill in the blank) are devious, hence your kind actions and thoughtful words must mean the opposite of what they seem.

This theoretical fear of uncertainty has thus led students of perception to assume that for experience to give us knowledge it needs to be mechanical in this paranoid sense of a step-by-step use of preexisting ideas. Anything mechanical, after all, ought to be foolproof. Unlike living creatures, the mechanisms that Descartes claims underlie our experience can never err. Those who consider uncertainty and ambiguity to be part of being alive have always viewed the Cartesian approach to experience with unease and concern (this is equally true of American pragmatist philosophers and European existential phenomenologists).[4] The Cartesian approach to experience has the scientific appeal of infallibility, but it has the serious drawback that it renders one incompetent in everyday life: one is either a blind believer in something for the sake of its clarity and alleged certainty or a blind cynic. But the Cartesian fear of uncertainty is not merely a philosophical theory; it has become a major cultural force in our world.

The retreat from the reality of life's uncertainty is nowhere more apparent than in the dominant tendencies of our so-called postindustrial culture. Every field from medicine to money making—even mysticism—searches for foolproof techniques. This search for certainty (and the parallel search for control) has extended to the realm of everyday practice as well. The modern workplace has become a vehicle for "information processing" in a way that offers disturbing parallels to Descartes's division of experience.

We can see this brought out strikingly in the course of an interview with a plant manager in Connecticut, reported by historian David Noble:

> With a colleague chiming in, he proudly described the elaborate procedure they had developed whereby every production change, even the most minor, had to be okayed by an industrial engineer. "We want absolutely no decisions made on the floor," he insisted; no operator was to make any change from the pro-

cess sheets without the written authorization of a superior. A moment later, however, looking out onto the floor from his glass-enclosed office, he reflected upon the reliability of the machinery and the expense of parts and equipment, and emphasized with equal conviction that "we need guys out there who can think."[5]

What the controllers want, in fact, is "guys who can think," but only in the sense of following the algorithms established in the work process by management—which are now being enshrined in office and industry computers throughout the country. Managers now reject personal experience, decision making, and judgment because of their persistent fear of uncertainty.

This need for guys who make no decisions but who, at the same time, "can think" has led to a shift in modern work relations, at least in the United States. Corporations have tended to swing between regimented, "top-down" control of production and some form of cooperative-work-group labor systems. The certainty pursued so diligently by managers in the control of their workers is, of course, a will-o'-the-wisp—hence, the constant shifting of management systems. Because of this control-obsessed mode of thinking in modern businesses and factories— even in schools—an independent thinker often functions as a monkey wrench thrown into the system rather than as a useful person to have around.

Descartes's division of "raw" sensory processes from "pure" ideas diminishes both kinds of awareness. This double-edged devaluation has long pervaded theory in epistemology and in psychology. But in recent decades everyday life has increasingly become subject to the same process of degradation. People with real, primary, hands-on skills (not derivative, information-handling skills, but skills in working with real things) are gradually being marginalized and separated from decision making in modern life, as I shall show in the next chapter. There is thus a connection between theories that treat experience as if it were a pure subjective state and the all-too-real and unpleasant situations many of us face because we are unable to use our experience to make important decisions about how we shall live.

How is the Cartesian degradation of experience entering our everyday lives? People who exercise control over other people have always feared the evil demon of uncertainty: at any moment, those on top of the social heap may be toppled down. What if Army privates no longer obeyed their sergeants? To forestall such mischief, these human controllers invented what Lewis Mumford dubbed the megamachine, the classic example of which was the work gangs on the pyramids.[6] Since the beginning of civilization, the ability to control the actions of one's subordinates has been essential for the achievement of certainty in practical matters. With the advent of modern automation and information technology, the need to construct megamachines from work gangs has receded, but not the obsession with control. As Mumford shows, technology is often used as a substitute for social relationships of control: what Pharaoh did with brute force, modern industrial managers often achieve by subtler means. The modern work gang consists of clerks who are enslaved to display terminals, rather than laborers enslaved to Pharaoh. Modern managers have attempted to convince us that this new form of servitude builds mental skills. New technologies and "modernization" are always packaged as skill-building innovations, but the reality has typically been the opposite.[7]

The nineteenth-century factory owners who fought against shortening the workday, thereby preventing the workhands (many of them children) from seeing daylight, and who created rules that forbade singing or conversation, were afraid of uncertainty. Like more recent devotees of free trade, they feared that any slacking off would undermine their competitiveness. The modern managers of service industries who force their employees to *avoid* genuine interactions with customers, requiring them instead to follow a preestablished script ("Have a good day, now, and thank you for . . . "), are afraid of the uncertainties of everyday social intercourse. Allowing employees to interact with customers on their own does not strike these controllers as a recipe for conviviality but as an example of a lack of management control. Fear of uncertainty has become widespread in recent years, and, increasingly, managers are relying on techniques and technologies for controlling subordinates in the hope of gaining certainty about both the details and the outcome of the work process. This intensification of constraint, aimed at the creation of predictability and certainty, is the essence of what I call the *machining of the mind*.[8]

In the industrial revolution, it was the movements of workers that were "machined" by being constrained to conform to predictable and controllable patterns, either through yoking workers to machinery or through the development of restrictive work rules. Until recent times and the advent of computerization, however, some amount of personal skill and experience in addition to (or even instead of) adherence to restrictive work rules were required for the satisfactory accomplishment of the majority of jobs.

In a remarkable study, based on a close analysis of small-arms manufacture in late nineteenth-century America, historian R. B. Gordon found that skilled workers actually made automated manufacture possible. This discovery is of special importance because small-arms manufacturing pioneered the use of interchangeable parts and other important aspects of assembly-line manufacture. Gordon found that interchangeability and standardization became possible only because highly skilled machinists could finish (properly modify) the machine-made products. The purely automated work process is, has been, and will continue to be, a myth: even in mechanized workplaces, personal skill, however invisible or undervalued, is essential.[9] We need to ask why skill is deemphasized by the mythmongers, who instead falsely emphasize the infallibility of mechanisms. Why is our contemporary culture so resistant to celebrating the fallible but real skills of people and so passionate in its celebration of mechanistic performance? This is not an issue of technology but one of philosophy and psychology.

The automated information processing, or "informatization," of our current economy involves even more standardization and mechanization than did the automation of assembly lines. Informatization requires a second, more stultifying level of control: the control of workers' mental processes. Once a workplace is run by means of information technology that is geared to an idealized model of the workplace and work process, then skilled workers become a *threat*. Any independent decision-making power of nonmanagement personnel becomes a daily source of uncertainty. Unless the *experience* (as well as the movements) of subordinates is "machined" into the management-produced model of the work process that has been encoded into the technology, the evil demon will be on the loose—the representation will no longer match what it is supposed to represent. Allowing independent decision making means taking the risk that the thing in the external world (the product) will not match the idea in the brain (the managerial plan). From a manager's perspective it is not the workers who machine and finish the products; it is the workplace that machines and finishes the workers. But why has our society—and especially why have our intellectuals and educators—succumbed to this narrow managerial perspective? Where are the defenders of everyday experience?

At every level of our information society, places of work are being "integrated" into the "information economy." The products of each working unit must therefore be molded to fit the needs of the information-processing systems. We now design work to fit abstract models of work processes in order for jobs to be put online. This means that an experienced worker, who may see a novel way to accomplish a goal, has to fit this new method into the software model, as well as into the work process. Because software and other information technology is always designed to work in a variety of processes, such new ideas typically require (expensive) modifications of the model. They are often rejected, therefore, even when they offer a better product or a chance to make the work go more smoothly. "We're sorry, but the computer doesn't allow us to do that," is the characteristic refrain of the postmodern world.

The much-vaunted decentralization and worker empowerment extolled by computer gurus has turned out to be hollow. Such empowering environments undoubtedly exist—but usually for the well-to-do and the self-employed. Increasingly, we are being asked to "reskill" ourselves solely to turn ourselves into information-cogs in complex computerized systems. (And especially so that our "efficiency" as cogs can be quantified.) This is demoralizing, to say the least. Those who expect technology to create new, and better, social relationships are naive and unhistorical. Just as technology is not the culprit when social relationships are poor, so it cannot in and of itself improve those relationships. This is something people have to do. The problem is not with information technology, which has many wonderful uses. The problem is that our culture has succumbed to a narrow managerial perspective concerning those uses—and many of the real, liberating potentials of these and other technologies are blocked by this managerial approach (what I am calling the machining of the mind), not by our machines.[10] Indeed, our postmodern world is thus achieving the reverse of what Dewey called for. Instead of using our information technology to create workplaces within which human experience can grow and thrive, we are using this technology to manufacture jobs that are often little more than glorified pigeonholes, with all opportunity for growth and reflection eliminated.

When an idealized representation fails to match reality, most of us believe that it makes sense to alter the representation. This is not the case within the Cartesian intellectual framework, nor is it the case within the practical framework of management, both of which invert common sense. In both management and Cartesian thinking the need for certainty is paramount, and certainty is often achieved by altering reality to fit the representation. Why alter the information processing in a production process, managers ask, when it is "easier" (for whom?) to change what the workers do and leave the process in place? Who has the time or money (or experience with the real process) to change a whole system? Besides, the workers can be made to adapt. It is usually expensive or impractical to make the information system adapt to the workers; thus, driven by fear of uncertainty, managers for the most part will not engage in the process of learning from how people have previously done a job: their mistakes and their successes. In a competitive marketplace, the time is never right for self-education.

Thus, the representations built into expensive technology become the new reality, tested neither for their validity nor for their cost-effectiveness, but dominant over every worker with whom they come in contact. (Interestingly, and in direct contrast to popular belief, there is little concrete evidence that computerization or informatization increases either efficiency or profitability, even in some industries, like banking, where one would most expect such increases.)[11] Furthermore, the jurisdiction of representation over reality increasingly extends to workers' minds; as information technology is integrated into workplaces, the information available to workers, and the actions they are allowed to take on the basis of that information, comes increasingly from computers and programs, not through the workers' own understanding of situations. To managers who view their primary task as the achievement of control, then, it apparently makes sense to mold reality to fit their ideas, regardless of the cost. Here again we see the opposite of what Dewey championed. Workers are not thought of as living creatures who must be nourished and grow but as parts of a system that must be shaped and fitted into place.

The separation of planning from activity is by no means limited to the workplace. As journalist James Howard Kunstler has shown in his history of modern American town planning, the automobile has effectively "automated" town planning. Traffic engineers have established a set of road patterns and rules to facilitate effective traffic flow, and these are often sold as a package to municipalities. "All the design matters are supposedly settled, and there has been little intelligent debate about them for years."[12] Few of the people affected (that is, most of us) discuss such basic issues of public life as how wide we should make streets or what kinds of buildings we should allow along what kinds of traffic routes.

Even among those few involved citizens who do debate building and street codes, the range of options has been tremendously narrowed by the a priori assumption that traffic flow is an unassailable public good. "Americans have been living car-centered lives for so long that the collective memory of what used to make a landscape or a townscape . . . humanly rewarding has nearly been erased. The culture of good place-making, like the culture of farming, or agriculture, is a body of knowledge and acquired skills. It is not bred in the bone, and if it is not transmitted from one generation to the next, it is lost."[13] As Kunstler goes on to show, in urban, rural, and suburban America, we are decreasingly capable of organizing environments that afford either a supportive surrounding for our work or a convivial surrounding for other forms of human interaction. Worse, few of us have had the experience of trying to make and shape such places; therefore, fewer and fewer of us cherish the hope that we might work toward the goal of making better places.

The ubiquitous complaint of modern life is that individuals feel less involved, out of control, isolated, and fearful (of both tangible and intangible things). These complaints do not have a single source but the widespread machining of the mind in schools, factories, offices, and the media probably plays a major role in fostering them. As a society, we are so used to searching for "solutions" (often imagined to be foolproof schemes—algorithms!) that most of us find it exceedingly scary to contemplate the possibility that the search itself lies at the root of our intellectual malaise. Can we recover our courage as individuals sufficiently to seek real, alive, dangerous, threatening experience? Can we recover our nerve as a society and encourage people to acquire and use their experience, even though they are bound to make mistakes and likely to fail in some endeavors? Surely we cannot, as a society, learn how to make better places of work or life quickly or without making mistakes. As individuals and as groups we need time and practice to recover our capacity to experience things for ourselves and to work collectively to further self-developed wisdom. In the absence of this recovery of experience, we are bound to oscillate between empty certainties and meaningless fragments of sensation; between endless cynicism and a futile series of empty beliefs. To be alive is to enjoy risks and to learn from mistakes—something most of our institutions deny to us on a daily basis. Can we come together to relearn the basic truth of human life that lived experience is central to our well-being?

# FOUR    The Degradation of Experience in the
Modern Workplace

There is an old joke about a person trapped in a fortune-cookie factory whose only hope for escape is to send out messages inside the cookies. It is disconcerting that the image conveyed by this joke—stripped of any pretense at humor—is nowadays often used to describe our lives. The notion that we are confined incommunicado and desperately seeking escape pervades our literature, philosophy, and even science. Claustrophobic images fill the talk of ordinary people, who complain about how trapped they feel at work, at home, and in their lives in general.[1]

Visions of anonymous protagonists struggling to deal with dark, confined places dominate the later fiction of Samuel Beckett, who is said to have given voice to our modern plight. It is significant that Beckett's often nameless protagonists frequently resort to measuring and mapping their peculiar confines—and even the people around them, as when the hero in *How It Is* measures his partner's body as they fornicate. As if Beckett were fleeing Descartes's evil demon, he worries about the impossibility of finding a listener or even someone to share his experience, to help him seek the shelter of certainty in ever-more claustrophobic circumstances. In the semi-autobiographical *Company,* Beckett puns of himself: "Even still in the timeless dark you find figures a comfort."[2] Numbers become a comfort because of their certainty in an otherwise absurd landscape.

Many philosophers have used this kind of Beckettian image to describe modern life. What is striking is that these philosophers are not complaining about our prisonlike existence but are celebrating it. In an attempt to articulate the lessons of artificial intelligence, the philosopher Daniel Dennett, for example, likens the processes of our minds to those of a person imprisoned in a place of flashing lights, dials, and levers who must try to figure out which button to push and which light to attend to without ever knowing what is occurring outside the prison.[3] This image of confinement in an absurd place, which originated with Franz Kafka's satires of bureaucratic mindlessness like *The Castle* (1954) and *The Trial* (1964), has migrated through literature and science to become a dominant metaphor for describing the mind in the late twentieth century. Far from helping us keep in contact with other people, modern technology—especially so-called information technology—has been used to reinforce and deepen the sense of division from others, of alienation from reality, and of the meaninglessness of events.[4]

People who feel they are trapped in meaningless places often respond by acting like machines. This is a mockery of Dewey's philosophy of growth: we put people in an environment in which only machines thrive, and the people grow to be like machines. In our late twentieth-century consumer society we have all found ourselves confronted with a person who is supposed to help us but cannot, and who justifies his failure by saying "the rules don't let me do it that way," as if he were no more than the automaton that in all probability he has been instructed to be. Whereas the nineteenth century was the machine age, our era is threatening to become the machined age.

Descartes and his evil demon tried to persuade us that *other* people were machines. But it has been the peculiarly sinister genius of our industrial culture to convince some people that *they themselves* are like machines. Although this feeling of mechanization characterizes many psychotic individuals, it is by no means limited to the insane; on the contrary, the notion that "I am a machine" is widely touted by philosophers and scientists. Many apparently sane, ordinary people also feel that they are becoming like machines, something about which they express both anger and resignation. These feelings derive from the widespread conditions of confinement, meaninglessness, and empty regularity in our lives. What our various corporate and institutional structures desire of most of us—in school, in the streets, in the workplace, even in public service—are obedience to rules and regulations, punctuality, and a self-imposed restraint, so that we develop a spontaneous aversion to individuality.

Henry David Thoreau, who loved the stolidity and patience of the New England woods, was driven to fury by the same characteristics in the men he saw around him in Massachusetts in the mid-1800s:

> The mass of men serve the state thus, not as
> men mainly but as machines, with their bodies.
> They are the standing army, and the militia,
> jailers, posse comitatus, etc. In most cases there
> is no free exercise whatever of judgment or of
> the moral sense; but they put themselves on a
> level with wood and earth and stones; and
> wooden men can perhaps be manufactured that
> will serve the same purpose as well. Such command no more respect than men of straw or a
> lump of dirt. Yet such as these even are commonly esteemed good citizens.[5]

Thoreau was thinking of modern political life and its degradation from a work of moral choice into a sequence of mechanical decisions. But the modern school or workplace is even more mechanized than the modern polity. In most cases, the good worker or student, like the good citizen, strives *not* to exercise independent judgment. Indeed, much of the trick of being a good worker or student is to do it with your body: to be in the right place and time, with the correct posture and attitude.

Because machinelike regularity, promptness, and precision are increasingly seen as proper and even virtuous attributes for people, it is hardly surprising that the study of "machine intelligence" flourishes. After all, if many of the activities in which people engage are mechanical, then machines ought to be able to perform these tasks equally well, or even better, as Thoreau suggested. For example, a *computer* used to be a person (almost always a woman) who worked with a large team of colleagues, who were all calculating mathematical tables for those twin pillars of modernity, gunnery (ballistics) and banks (actuarial tables and the like). This kind of drudge work was what electronic computers first succeeded in automating—and what they still do best.

Many commentators have concluded from such instances of successful automation that artificial intelligence is a reality or at least a soon-to-be-achieved possibility. If machines can perform our tasks, should we not consider them intelligent? Many would assume that the answer to this question is "yes." But should we not heed Thoreau and ask, "Will machines do the work of the real people or just the wooden ones?" In which situations is it desirable to eliminate the drudgery of people and give machines the work, and in which is it important to emphasize the meaningful aspects of work and the importance of human experience in that work? In the 1980s the philosopher John Searle contrived an amusing way of showing how the mechanical simulation of human performance does not necessarily prove that machines are intelligent.

Like Beckett's later fiction and the joke about the fortune-cookie factory, Searle's argument begins with an image of imprisonment: an English-speaking person is placed in a room with no way out.[6] There is nothing much to do, but the room contains a dispenser that shoots out papers with written marks on them, what appears to be an interpretation book or manual, and materials for writing. Because she is bored, the victim of this imprisonment studies the writing coming in and finds that she does not understand it, although she suspects that it may be Chinese ideograms. On scrutinizing the manual available to her, she finds that the ideograms (if that is what they are) on the pieces of paper are also in the manual, with what might be English equivalents. Our prisoner cannot be sure that the marks are Chinese—or that the English words are their translations—for the good reason that she is completely ignorant of the Chinese language. Having nothing better to do, she decides she might as well take each paper and write the English words from her manual next to the "corresponding" symbols on the paper. At this point she notices what might be a mail slot in the wall of her room, and, for fun, she places some of her English writing in it.

From the outside, this prison looks like a "black box" for translating Chinese ideograms into English words (because that is what all those marks and the manual, in fact, are). Someone who did not know that a person was inside might even think that this was a computer for translating Chinese-language fortunes into English-language fortunes (because, unbeknownst to our prisoner, all the Chinese ideograms are fortunes and sayings).

Searle's argument about this prison (although he uses the euphemism *room*) is simple. Even a person who knew no Chinese could turn ideograms into English words. Perhaps, after a long while, the prisoner might even learn Chinese, but certainly knowledge of Chinese is unnecessary to start the process. When we find that a computer program has been developed for turning Chinese ideograms into English equivalents, therefore, we had better not assert that the computer "understands" Chinese, or that it is "translating." Since a human being can accomplish these things without either understanding or translating, a computer can certainly do so as well. In Thoreau's language, the fact that a machine can do the job of a wooden man (or woman) is in itself insufficient evidence that the machine can think or is intelligent.

Although Searle's argument is a strong one, it is weakened by being based on a thought experiment, a purely hypothetical case. Yet a number of recent trends in the use of information technology could be used to make the same points. Searle's imprisoned translator resembles many people who find themselves trapped in rote jobs, using technological devices to mediate between two steps in a complex information process over which they have no control, about which they have little general knowledge, and concerning which they have scant interest.

### IN THE FORTUNE-COOKIE FACTORY

Looked at from the worker's point of view, the fundamental goal of modern management is to make all jobs resemble the one in Searle's prison. As far as managers are concerned, workers should always follow explicit rules and job descriptions (the manual), regardless of what they think a situation calls for. When exceptional situations arise, the worker should fetch a supervisor, not resolve the matter herself. (This procedure is so annoying to customers and consumers that some companies have created "exception workers" to monitor and handle problem cases.) Hungarian social theorist Georg Lukács long ago explained that "rationalization" in work meant "being able to predict with precision all the results to be achieved."[7] In the competitive environment of large modern corporations an emphasis on regularity and precision is considered essential to economic efficiency. But Lukács also saw what modern managers do not seem to have seen: that rote work is spiritually deadening. The rationalized, explicit procedure becomes the job, and personal experience becomes only a *deviation* from the proper course—as Lukács put it, workers "appear increasingly as mere sources of error."[8] Living things are always out of place in machine shops.

Our modern workplaces and technological systems are designed to be mind-deadening. Terrified of the evil demons of independent thought and experience, managers insist on systematizing procedures so that they can (and should?) be followed unthinkingly. When an error does occur, we all blame the human operator for creating the problem. When an American high-technology naval cruiser blew an Iranian passenger plane out of the sky in the mid-1980s, the press kept wondering how the mistake could have occurred. A sailor with good binoculars would probably have seen that the oncoming plane was a passenger, not fighter, jet, but the radar operators decided it was a potential enemy plane. Are these sailors to blame for their stupid, unnecessary, and deadly error? After all, they were *trained* to rely on the instruments and to *avoid* using their eyes or binoculars, much less their own judgment. They had learned their lessons well—and the result was a catastrophe.

Whenever disaster occurs we are told that the machines worked well but the people did not. No one ever asks whether either the machines or the people should have been put into the region of potential danger, or whether working with the machine and following managerial guidelines have depleted whatever judgment the people might have had. We note that the worker deviated from procedure, but we do not inquire whether the procedure was sensible to begin with.

Work requires experience and skill, especially in those cases where individual workers are involved in many phases of production, because it is necessary for involved workers to understand the meaning of what they are doing at each phase of the process. Involved workers can use their skill and tools to transform nature according to a plan. But whereas "in handicrafts and manufactures the worker makes use of a tool, in the factory, the machine makes use of [the worker]," as Karl Marx so tellingly put it.[9] When the "machinery" consists of information-processing technology, then the workers' experience and understanding have to come under the control of a "rationalized" process. One human cog in a large system of information technology cannot be allowed to question the process. In the nineteenth century, work processes were redesigned to adapt to the needs of steam- and coal-driven machinery. In our day, work processes are being redesigned to fit the needs of computers. Moreover, because computers are now widely used in service and sales industries, not merely in production, almost all transactions in our society are being machine-fit to the needs of computers. Ask yourself, from your own experience, how much effort is being expended on making the worlds of manufacturing and sales computer-compatible. Now ask yourself how much effort is being expended upon making the world safer or healthier for its human inhabitants. The contrast is disconcerting, to say the least.

The specialization of work to serve the needs of machinery changes workers from people who regulate tools according to their purposes into devices for maintaining the flow of the machinery. The specialization of work to serve the needs of information technology changes workers from people who use their experience to facilitate the accomplishment of goals into devices for maintaining the flow of (automated) information. Excessive emphasis on such specialization is harmful: the specialized industrial worker has neither a product nor a general skill to share with others; the specialized information worker does not even have a unique personal work experience to share. This constriction of the work experience could be offset by greater opportunities for experience during schooling or in leisure time—but, as I shall discuss below, these domains also emphasize secondhand over primary experience.

Human cultures are based on the conflicts and harmonies that emerge when different people, with different needs, experiences, products, and skills, interact.[10] The absence of shared meanings in modern American society so loudly decried by conservative critics of modern education like Allan Bloom is not a result of our educational system but of our daily lives, which systematically discourage the development of genuinely shared meanings, whether through cooperation or conflict.[11] Dewey's ideal of the school as an environment for supporting eagerness to learn, in both individuals and groups, has never been tried. Since his day, schools have increasingly been modeled on large-scale factories, and students are becoming "operators," with a series of tasks to learn, perform, and master. The perennial and popular conservative complaints about schooling in the United States thus take on the pernicious form of criticizing the victims (the students) for being unable to prevent their victimization. We place students in environments that do not support learning and then complain that they are deficient in learning. We offer them little reason to care about what they learn and then behave as if dumping megabytes into their brains will spontaneously start those brains working. As a society we are willing to spend billions of dollars on information superhighways, but we begrudge every penny spent to fix up schools to make the environment a little more appealing for the teachers and students who spend their time there.

This mechanization and fragmentation of experience constitutes in itself an attack on our cultural heritage for, as William Morris long ago noted, personal skills are the fundamental component of all cultures: "The skill and force of the workman, the craftsman, . . . is most truly the heritage handed down to us by countless years of tradition. . . . Yet this precious heritage our society of commercial privilege wastes lightheartedly as if it were a part of the nature of things to make the worst of that which is the best of things, the token and reward of the world's progress, the hope of its future."[12] It is striking that Morris's rhetoric is so jarring to modern ears. We rarely, if ever, think of "progress" in terms of people and their development. Indeed, progress as we have been taught to think of it is often something that leaves people, their experience, and their skills behind.

As Dewey emphasized, the ability of persons to become independently skilled, autonomous, and useful selves should not be thought of as an intrinsic self-sufficiency in the sense of being able to do all things on one's own—nor is this a useful goal, unless one plans on being imprisoned in a fortune-cookie factory. Human autonomy is better seen as a kind of self-adequacy, in which one can make a contribution within the give and take of community life. Again, as Dewey emphasized, experience is a process; a person who is experienced can join with others in creating a group process that facilitates the experience of other members of the group. To do this requires the development of skill and experience sufficient to give one the capacity to take one's place among others. Those who bemoan the ever-increasing degradation of our cultural and civic heritage might do better than pointing accusing fingers at educators; they might ask instead whether the daily grind of our lives is not itself inimical to the pursuit of *any* progressive cultural or civic expression.[13] Our schools do not encourage independent thought or expression. (Some would say they dare not do so!) Our workplaces have long been organized to thwart both skill development and collaborative endeavor. Our entertainments require little more than turning on and tuning in. Is this an environment that will encourage either individual or civic flourishing? It seems unlikely, but let us not single out the victims of this process for special blame.

Workers' mechanical skills were machined by slide rule and stopwatch in the heyday of "scientific management." Now, with the ever-present computer, our mental skills are also being machined. Technology theorist James Beniger notes that modern management constantly has to face "the one shortcoming common to all [control systems] based on human brains: independence of purpose."[14] Fortunately—or so Beniger thinks—

control processes, like production processes, can now be "rationalized," thanks to information technology. Although managers and intellectual leaders invariably introduce computer and information technology as something that offers intellectual challenge and stimulation to workers, stimulation, as we have seen, is neither the rationale for nor the result of the technology's introduction. Rather, the ability of information technology to present highly controlled information to workers allows managers to constrain, control, and monitor their responses more efficiently. Managers can thus both design all the phases of the information flow in a production process (or even a service process) and ensure that only their design is followed—and they can identify the workers who do not follow the model.[15] If we could all do our jobs in the manner of Searle's trapped fortune writer, or a daydreaming cashier with an invincible arm for laser scanning, that would be fine—indeed, it would be ideal, because workers would not be tempted to "interfere" with the information flow.

There are many people who resist this view of information technology and claim that, far from constricting our minds, computers can facilitate and improve our intellectual abilities. This positive view of information technology is widespread among academics and intellectuals, few of whom have ever had to drudge eight hours a day within an information system not of their own devising—and that monitors their work rate, penalizing them for poor performance. The issue is not one of technology but of what Lewis Mumford called technics: how we use the technology. Under some conditions, computer technology can become mind enhancing. Academics and writers—who more or less control their working time and are not being monitored to see how many keystrokes they make in an hour—tend to find at least some of their work facilitated by computerization. The issue here is not what can happen in special cases, however, but what actually happens in most workplaces and schools. The controversies over whether, in principle, computers can think or whether, in principle, automation can benefit workers, are moot, a legacy of the universalizing philosophy we would do well to cast aside. The point that needs attention is what happens to the majority of the people who are being forced to interpret their daily lives in categories imposed upon them by other people (managers) through the medium of the increasingly constraining technology of their work. The problem lies with the people who are establishing the uses to which the technology is being put—and with our intellectuals and educators, who by and large have acceded to the managerial perspective that makes such terrible use of the technology.

Searle's image of imprisonment is a fairly good model of how ordinary people deal with the increasingly common situation of being trapped inside someone else's information system: here is a more-or-less arbitrary system of rules that commands me and over which I have no control; if I have to, I guess I can learn them—and I can spend my workday thinking of other things. For instance, a dental-claims operator says: "The computer system is supposed to know all the limitations [on claims], which is great, because I no longer know them."[16] There is a sense among people in these situations that the meaning has been sucked out of what they do and injected into the "system" (or the computer). Because an individual no longer performs a complete operation, it is difficult for one person to learn the overall job or to evaluate his own performance (or that of the system): "I used to [know what was going on], but now I don't know half the things I used to. I feel that I have lost it—the computer knows more. I am pushing buttons."[17] Why would individuals in these circumstances want to understand the intricacies of their workplace's "system"? Why would a cashier ever want to read a bar code?

Managers' fear of uncertainty and their search for reliability through repetition have thus led many of us to a perilous place. We are surrounded by information systems that are studded with workers, like raisins in a Christmas pudding. As we all know, from the constant petty interruptions of our lives as workers or consumers, these systems are by no means as foolproof as we would like to believe (there are legions of gremlins about, if not the evil demon himself), and they are often "down" or malfunctioning. Those who operate the systems are rarely capable of performing its tasks through their own efforts. Their experience has shrunk to the narrowest confines, as in Searle's story. These people understand their position within the system and little else. But knowing one's place in an information processing network rarely, if ever, helps one figure out how to get the whole job done. Like Searle's imprisoned translator, operators within the system have little or no comprehension of how the things they do fit into the larger procedure. They are forced to rely almost exclusively on indirect experience, based on manipulated and transmitted information. But experience is a living thing, and it thrives only through exercise and practice. The workers who are trapped like Searle's translator find that their capacity for firsthand experience—and the judgment that comes from it—is constantly curtailed by their surroundings and, hence, tends to wither.

### DIVIDED LIVES, SEGMENTED WORK

The moral of Searle's fable is thus not that machines cannot understand what they do. After all, it is (remotely) possible that some fancy, conscious machine placed in the fortune-cookie factory would be just as bored and alienated as you or I. Rather, the point of Searle's fable is that as a culture we have been misled into thinking that reliability, rapidity, and repeatability are the hallmarks of intelligence. There is no good reason to make this assumption. We ought instead to consider the alternatives. As cross-cultural psychologist Barbara Rogoff writes: "Indigenous concepts of intelligence vary widely, with some behaviors valued at opposite extremes. . . . Ugandan villagers associate intelligence with adjectives such as slow, careful, and active, whereas Ugandan teachers and Westernized groups associate intelligence with the word speed."[18]

The emphasis on speed, repetition, and certainty that pervades modern life has blinded us to the shortcomings of these virtues. Wisdom emerges from the kinds of experiences that typify complex human behavior: change, uncertainty, the making of difficult choices, and the like. Our civilization fancies that it exalts individuality, but what we really honor is the search for rapidity and certainty—at the expense of wisdom. Our schools and workplaces—even our entertainments—rarely emphasize the desirability of uncertainty and difficult choices, and few of us receive consistent opportunities to test ourselves in complex situations (and, yes, to make mistakes). Far too many of us have been sold on a fast-food view of the world: we want a few easy, fast choices, with quick fixes always available. We have chosen to be certain and speedy rather than to be wise.[19]

Stated abstractly, the virtues of speed, repetition, and certainty sound desirable but in specific contexts—like Searle's fable—their limits become clear. When everyday processes take on the repetitive precision of an algorithm, they lose their meaning. When these repetitive processes are further rarefied by becoming part of a preestablished information-processing system, we eliminate almost all the meaning of direct everyday experience. One cannot learn from experience when that experience is so routinized that nothing in it varies. Indeed, we might even speak of a complete loss of experience, as cultural theorist Walter Benjamin prophesied in the dark days before World War II, when he warned that the mechanization of daily life undermined the appreciation of variation and spontaneity that was essential to creativity.[20] Those of us who are trapped in the fortune-cookie factory have no stories to tell. We wish to get out because we have little chance of doing anything worth sharing—worth telling about—until we do. But how did we come to be trapped? As Dewey long ago emphasized, the causes of our metaphysical predicament are largely economic.

Dewey argued that one of the key forces that acts to degrade experience is the division of labor.[21] By this Dewey did not mean specialization, however, but, more particularly, a specialization in which physical and mental work are separated— something that is increasingly common in our information-based economy. As Dewey suspected, the division of labor in modern society has two phases. In the first, the work is divided into simple, short, rote processes. In the second, the *workers* are segregated; different groups of workers perform different functions in the overall work process. These two phases of the division of labor have different psychological and social consequences.

The segmenting of work into short, meaningless operations is widely regarded as the major aim of the division of labor. Social psychologist Michael Argyle notes that modern work cycles are often repetitions of processes that last less than a minute.[22] Thus, a worker might well repeat a procedure nearly 100 times an hour, eight hours a day. As Adam Smith explained, this form of the division of labor was created in response to the market. When there is a large market for a product, significant advantages accrue to segmenting the work process into subtasks or even into the minuscule labor molecule of the modern workplace. When I make a peanut-butter-and-jelly sandwich for myself, I might assemble the desired items in a haphazard order. When making sandwiches for a family of ten or more, I am more likely to line up the bread first, then the peanut butter, then the jelly, and proceed systematically.

Adam Smith is mostly remembered for his praise of the efficiencies produced by the division of labor. This is probably because he discusses them in the first few pages of a large and dense book. But buried away in his discussion of the need for public education is a remarkable analysis of the drawbacks to the division of labor—drawbacks that are, for the most part, psychological in nature. The passage is worth quoting at length:

> In the progress of the division of labour, the employment of the . . . great body of the people, comes to be confined to a very few simple operations; frequently to one or two. But the understandings of the greater part of men are necessarily formed by their ordinary employments. The man whose whole life is spent in performing a few simple operations, of which the effects, too are, perhaps, always the same, or very nearly the same, has no occasion to exert his understanding, or to exercise his invention in finding out expedients for removing difficulties which never occur. He naturally loses, therefore, the habit of such exertion, and generally becomes as stupid and ignorant as it is possible for a human creature to become. The torpor of his mind renders him, not only incapable of relishing or bearing a part in any rational conversation, but of conceiving any generous, noble, or tender sentiment, and consequently of forming any just judgment concerning many even of the ordinary duties of private life. . . . His dexterity at his own particular trade seems, in this manner, to be acquired at the expense of his intellectual, social, and martial virtues. But in every . . . civilized society this is the state into which the labouring poor, that is, the great body of the people, must necessarily fall, unless government takes some pains to prevent it.[23]

Smith, who is of course held up as the greatest proponent of laissez-faire policy (in which government does nothing), feels strongly that it is a government's duty to ameliorate the malign effects of the division of labor, a division Smith saw as inevitable in a modern capitalist society.

The extent of markets has grown astronomically since Smith's day, and the corresponding segmentation of labor has also grown. The short and simple tasks of weavers and pin makers (which Smith had in mind) are as symphonies compared to the ditties of labor allowed to modern assembly-line workers. Since Smith's day, belief in the value of public education has grown, although we rarely hear Smith's argument for it: that general education is necessary to prevent or at least lessen the brutalization of workers forced to perform segmented tasks. Worse, it is nowadays a commonplace to hear arguments that the value of education is that it prepares students for work (a usual accompaniment of these arguments is the fear that education in the United States does not prepare us well enough). When we think about the kind of work that the majority of public-school students will graduate to do, it is difficult to take such arguments seriously, for only a fraction of the students will take jobs that require a broad-ranging educational background. It is astonishing that the many—apparently sincere—advocates of "better schooling for a better world" seem not to have looked around sufficiently to realize that most people nowadays work at jobs that require little education, except in the sense of instruction on how to conform to a set program. Education that prepares the student for segmented labor would be as boring and repetitive as the divided labor itself (as, sadly, some of our education proves to be). Perhaps we should heed Smith's prescient warning and think of teaching people how to compensate themselves for the deadening effects of modern life through some form of cultural activity.[24] Better yet, perhaps we should rethink our readiness to succumb to the blandishments of highly divided labor.

The second phase of the division of labor leads to what I have called the machining of the mind. Once work has been segmented and the workers have begun to adapt to the work cycles, the need for systematicity arises. Uniformity and reliability of product are also functions of the extent of the market. Managers attempt to ensure uniformity by developing new controls for the production process. Any deviations from the rules of the managers—even deviations that improve the product—are seen as problematic and threatening (a manifestation of the evil demon). In a highly segmented work process workers become tools, and if tools do not perform consistently, they are of no use. Many technology theorists and workplace designers would agree with technology theorist H. H. Rosenbrock's suggestion that "human beings who are to fulfill the role of programmable devices must be standardized, because otherwise a different program will be needed for each worker."[25]

In those few cases where workers were allowed to be involved in the planning and organizing of their work, they have shown considerable skill and enthusiasm. At General Electric's plant for making airplane parts in Lynn, Massachusetts, worker involvement was sought for the reorganization of the production process. The shop-floor machinists were able to make their jobs more productive in part by eliminating unnecessary layers of management, such as the foremen. Upon reviewing this successful experiment at the end of a year, the top management of General Electric decided to eliminate worker input and revert to the previous system. A worker-organized plant could not be fit into the transnational flow of information and control as easily as a management-run plant—and, apparently, no amount of increased efficiency or profitability would serve to make it worthwhile to opt for worker control. A standardized assembly line, it seems, is all that G.E. wants to bring to life.[26]

The standardization of workers requires more than segmenting the labor process, it also involves separating planning from execution. That is, all aspects of planning and evaluation of the work process must be kept strictly separated from the carrying out of the plans. Only then can the execution of the plans be reliable—it now resembles the carrying out of an algorithmic computation on a computer. Managers react to the fear of uncertainty by saving all planning and evaluation functions for themselves, which further reduces workers to tools for implementing a process.

In the modern workplace the worker is set short, rote tasks that have had the meaning drained out of them. It is emphatically not true that segmenting and standardizing the work are the most efficient ways to ensure production. On the contrary, it is only *because* planning is separated from execution that the standardization of workers is perceived as a necessity. If workers retained some say in planning and evaluation, standardization would be disastrous, as all sorts of variable and unpredictable problems would be likely to go unsolved. As Rosenbrock notes, "People differ in their skill and experience," but in the present-day segmented and separated workplace, "none of this can be called upon. The standard man or woman for whom tasks are designed must have no more ability or skill than can reliably be found in every worker. . . . Tasks must be simplified so they can be learned in the shortest possible time. . . . Taken to its extreme, this attitude leads to the view that many industrial tasks are most suited to the abilities of the mentally handicapped."[27]

The first phase of the division of labor segments work and degrades workers by deskilling them, assigning them to rote jobs. The second phase of the division of labor standardizes or "rationalizes" work and degrades workers by draining thought, planning, and autonomy from their daily experience. Together, these tendencies act to create an environment that seriously degrades human experience, providing less direct experience and more indirect, processed experience, in which the worker cannot be expected to expand his or her possibilities—the opposite of Dewey's environment that encourages human flourishing.

### THE MECHANIZATION OF LABOR

The division of labor has created a number of forces that contribute to the mechanization of skill and experience. The segmentation of jobs, which helps in the production of a large number of standardized products for an extensive market, condemns the workers to boredom and alienation from the job. Daydreaming and drug use are common responses to this phase of the division of labor, as has been found time and again by researchers. In the second phase, where planning and evaluation are separated from the execution of tasks, the result is a *standardized producer*—who offers no threat to the work process.

Together, these phases lead to what I call the menuization of the world. Increasingly, workers, consumers, and students are faced not with real choices (choices that emerge from the planning and evaluation of a project) but with choices from what systems designers call a menu of options. That is, the options are preset (and tend to consist of segmented tasks); the only choice is which option to pick. It is possible, in some situations, to move outside the menu and ask for real choices, but there is usually a serious cost to doing so. That is, real choices are increasingly expensive in terms of money, time, and control. We are thus creating a world in which action itself—which involves open-ended, thoughtful choice—is disappearing, to be replaced by "choices" among a small set of preestablished alternatives. Real action includes experience and involves encountering one's surroundings and acting to change one's relations with things and people. Modern schools, workplaces, and even forms of entertainment tend to prevent such autonomous acts and encounters. Instead of opportunities for action and experience, we are offered a menu of options and a lecture on the value of freedom of choice.

Given the divorce of our intellectual tradition from everyday life, it has been relatively easy for commentators to treat these major social trends as regrettable but not central to our understanding of human life. Daniel Dennett's *Elbow Room* (1984), for example, a book on the problem of free will, describes a division between the "gifted" people in the populace and the rest.[28] The gifted people are endowed with the ability to argue rationally and evaluate circumstances according to those arguments, and they, of course, are the people whom we ask to run things. Nowhere in the book is it mentioned that the majority of us, gifted or not (including, yes, even many academics), have little say in the planning processes that affect our lives, such as the plans made by corporate directors, city, county, and state managers, and others. It is a mixed blessing to be able to reason in a world where reasoning is, if tolerated at all, systematically ignored. Rorty's utopia at least has the advantage of honesty: his gifted and isolated ironists do not fool themselves into thinking they run things.

The automation of "manual" jobs, on the other hand, succeeded because managers created work processes that separated the planning of the activities and their execution.[29] The next step in automation, the mechanization of "intellectual" labor, is rapidly proceeding via the creation of workplaces in which not only human activity but also human experience is divided.

A remarkable example of this transformation of work from meaningful and thoughtful action into mindless menu-checking is the evolution of government social work, as described by journalist Barbara Garson. As Garson says, social work "was the right kind of work for my fellow Berkeley students who pinned IBM registration cards onto their chests to declare *Do not fold, spindle, or mutilate*. They demanded to be treated as individuals, not numbers."[30] But social work has been and is still being divided into simple component tasks ("actions," such as registering a client for food stamps), and both evaluation and decision making have been largely removed from individual social workers. The irony of creating social workers who cannot evaluate clients is not lost on the workers themselves, although perhaps it has escaped those who planned the system. Standardization of workers and systematicity of output are ensured because evaluation and planning are now embodied in rules and regulations, which are themselves embodied in computer programs.

As a result of this division of labor, social workers are now essentially menu operators. They serve as human "intakes" to a computer system that categorizes (some would say pigeonholes) clients in order to calculate their benefits. Social workers see clients, it would seem, because no one has yet devised a way for the clients themselves to enter the pertinent information into the computers. Social workers in the Massachusetts office studied by Garson are evaluated (and paid) entirely in terms of how many actions (menu choices) they perform—they are neither paid nor given positive evaluations for talking to or counseling clients. Moreover, they are constantly monitored to make sure that they do not deviate from the procedure and start counseling people.[31]

Sharing information and giving advice has thus been banished from the official world of many social workers! This is not to say that they are *forbidden* to counsel clients, but they can expect to be penalized for taking a human interest in the raw material (people) that presents itself to the welfare office to be processed (receive help). "The way it is now," said one of Garson's informants, "you're not a social worker, you're an FAW [Financial Assistance Worker]. If you take ten minutes out to help one kid in a family, you're gonna fall behind."

Decreased discretionary power goes hand in hand with decreased knowledge. In the office studied by Garson, social workers no longer worked out a number of the financial calculations that had previously been their responsibility. This meant that "newer workers who'd never done the calculations themselves couldn't estimate for a client that cutting her rent from

$200 to $150 might in fact make the family poorer [by causing her food stamps to be eliminated]." Garson frequently heard, "I can't answer that question. The computer will let you know." I leave it up to the reader to decide how common such statements are getting to be.

One of the more startling revelations in Garson's study involved a manager who was so perturbed at the new system that he urged the union to engage in a "work to rule" job action. He argued that following the rules of the system precisely would cause it to collapse. For example, a social worker could meet his or her monthly quota of actions in the first three weeks of every month and then take a week's paid vacation. Unfortunately, working to rule would also mean not explaining to families how cheaper rent or taking a part-time job might jeopardize their benefits, something most social workers are unwilling to do. Ironically, the only way to do the job the system was created for is to undermine the system.

In Britain, where some unions have a tradition of using such tactics as work to rule, institutions like the Post Office have been paralyzed by the chaos that emerges when all the workers take all the work rules seriously and try to follow them. This is perhaps the best evidence that many rules are not the embodiments of the most rational and efficient work procedures but are instead vehicles for maintaining the division of labor and control over workers. Garson's manager argued that the goal of the new system "is to take every aspect of [human] judgment away from the welfare worker and have it made inside the machine—which is to say, at a higher level. The aim is to restrict discretion and intervention (usually pro-client) by workers in the local office."

The ability of some managers to enforce the strict segregation of experience from decision making, and the widespread acceptance of this distinction in modern epistemologies, must not be taken as evidence that this distinction is a basic psychological fact.[32] The existence of mechanical automation shows that job activities can be divided into managing and doing. The existence of information-processing automation shows that workers can be divided into the providers of raw data and the people who are allowed to exercise judgment upon those data. But what can be done is one thing, and what ought to be done is another.

We know that these machined situations are abhorrent to the majority of people in them and that they are often actively resisted. To respond systematically to these degradations of modern life, however, we need a form of experience that celebrates and promotes nonmachined awareness, in which experience and judgment are inseparable. I am attempting here to make explicit what is implicit in so many critiques of the modern condition: that machined experience is limited and limiting. Machined experience is not merely one form of life among others; it is not a choice that an individual can make about how to live. Machined experience is the product of institutional realities in the modern world that restrict the possibilities available to most people for psychological growth. This reduced and indirect form of experience is constraining, especially when it comes to the important task of using experience to make ourselves into the kind of person we wish to be. Machined experience cannot be defended as a personal or even a social choice because it encompasses a system that can exist only if few people have a complete array of choices. To understand how we can break out of the constraints of this indirect, circumscribed, and machined experience, we need to explore what a richer, more direct kind of experience would involve.

# FIVE   Sharing Experience

All animals are aware of at least some of the meanings and values of their surroundings. Even simple animals—earthworms, for example—show a discriminating appreciation of those facts of their habitat that are relevant to their lives. Earthworms may not worry about the meaning of life or their social successes and failures, but, with their soft skins, they are demonstrably acute at detecting the relative scratchiness of soils.[1] Meaningful information about the relation of an animal to its surroundings is available in all environments. Experience comes from finding and using this information, and experience goes through refinements that occur in the process of information pickup through practice and learning.

Where traditional theories of experience place meanings inside the head—as a process of constructing meanings from meaningless inputs—the ecological approach to experience places meaning in the environment. What counts as meaningful is what the world affords to the observer, for good or ill. These "affordances of the environment," as James Gibson calls them, are a function of the structure of the environment, aspects of an animal's ecological niche. Just as rocky soil may be too scratchy for earthworms, so extreme desert conditions often prove fatal to humans. An organism's experience of these affordances derives from its changing needs, interests, and activities. With the proper protection and precautions, the interested human can survive a jaunt in the desert. In this view, the process of acquiring meanings is not a form of subjective consultation but an active process in which an animal seeks something from its world.

The kind of experience obtainable from looking and listening is direct, or firsthand. But much of our human experience is not so isolated and individualistic: we learn about our world in the company of other people, with whom we frequently interact. We should therefore be careful to distinguish firsthand experience from secondhand, in which the information we rely on to learn about the world has, in one way or another, been modified, selected, or produced by another person. Because traditional Western theories of perception start from the idea that finding meanings involves some form of inner or subjective consultation, they often make firsthand experience into a caricature of secondhand experience—as if one were interacting with an inner self. On the other hand, this subjectivism makes it difficult to understand how secondhand experience actually works, for doesn't one always have to convert another person's information into one's own internal meaningful medium? If this is true, however, all dialogue with others becomes a variant on talking to oneself. But of course we can and do share our experience with each other. Given its confusions about primary versus secondary experience, Western thought has always had difficulty accounting for this human ability to share awareness.

The ecological psychology I develop here sees both first- and secondhand experience as important, although they differ in significant but complementary ways. Firsthand experience involves using information obtained autonomously. Secondhand experience typically derives from situations that also offer some form of firsthand experience, but what makes the experience secondhand is that one has to take information that is selected by someone else. In face-to-face interactions, for example, one perceives at second hand, through the media of language and gesture, yet one also directly observes the person who is doing the gesturing or speaking. Even when secondhand information comes from something as impersonal as the process of reading, one still needs the firsthand perception of the marks on the paper or the blobs on the computer screen in order to extract the meaning of the words. In spite of these connections between second- and firsthand experience, secondhand experience still carries an important limitation not found in firsthand experience. When one is examining the world for oneself there is no limit to the scrutiny—one can look as carefully as one wishes, and one can always uncover new information.[2] But this is emphatically not the case with secondhand information. A description of a scene—even a photograph or a videotape of a scene—necessarily *selects* information; unless one is able to investigate the original scene, there will always be an externally imposed limit to one's scrutiny of it. This selection makes secondhand experience crucial to the sharing of experience, but what is gained in the ability to focus and point another's attention to something is lost in comprehensiveness and openness.

### KEEPING IN TOUCH WITH THE WORLD

Imagine you are sitting next to a friend who is driving down a long, straight, deserted highway. Ahead there is a mountain, and there are white guardrails along both sides of the road. Now imagine what the pattern of light and form on the windshield in front of you looks like as you are moving—not the terrain you see out the front window but the pattern of forms that are, as it were, projected onto the windshield. The mountain toward which you are heading is at the center of this array of

optical forms, and it does not move as long as your path along the road is straight, although the image of the mountain increases in size (perhaps only slightly, if the mountain is far away). At the edge of the pattern on the windshield will be the images of the guardrails, which sweep by, seeming to gain in size and speed, until they pass out of sight behind you. Between the mountain and the guardrails is the image of the road surface, projected up onto the windshield. These bits of optical texture also sweep along, gaining in size and speed until they pass out of sight as well.

This flowing array of images characterizes a law of nature—a law that we all observe but rarely think about, just as we all observe gravity and rarely think about it. When a terrestrial animal moves, it is surrounded by a flowing *optic array* that contains this internal structure, dubbed *perspective flow* by its discoverer, James Gibson.[3] (Readers who have spent any time in video arcades playing games that involve racing cars or flying airplanes or even spaceships will recognize these perspective-flow patterns.) Perspective flow has two poles. These are the points that do not move but out of which all motion and increase in size appear to arise. The point in front is called the *focus of expansion* because objects at it appear to expand. (Look again at the mountain toward which you are heading; notice how it is growing in apparent size, even if very slowly, and observe that the growth is symmetrical around a particular point, which is the focus of expansion). Directly behind the focus of expansion is the *focus of contraction,* a point toward which all the optical motions converge, and at which all objects shrink. (You have to look out the rear window to see this, of course.) The *lines of longitude* connecting these two poles are the *sweep lines* of all the optical projections in the field of view, such as those from the posts of the guardrails or from the road surface. These increase in size and speed as they approach the midway position between the two poles (a kind of imaginary equator), after which they begin to decrease in speed and size as they move toward the focus of contraction.

Perspective flow is a law of nature because it occurs wherever and whenever an animal moves. The focus of expansion is always the point toward which one is heading. If the road curves, "placing" the mountain off to the left, the focus of expansion will shift to the right, to specify the point toward which the car is moving. Just as we intuitively make use of gravity for many of our activities, such as bouncing a basketball, so we make use of this optical law to control our actions. For instance, in approaching an object we move so that the image of the object coincides with the focus of expansion, and we keep the focus of expansion there, and magnify it, until the object begins to fill our field of view. To stay on course, we must make sure that the image of the object is magnified symmetrically (that is, the whole image expands uniformly, not just on one side). "There are many rules involving magnification," wrote Gibson, listing a few: "To permit scrutiny, magnify the patch in the array to such a degree that details can be looked at. To manipulate something graspable, magnify the patch to such a degree that the object is within reach. . . . To kiss someone, magnify the face-form, if the facial expression is amiable, so as almost to fill the field of view. (It is absolutely essential to keep one's eyes open so as to avoid collision. It is also wise to learn to discriminate [the subtle information that specifies] amiability.)"[4] Whimsical as this suggestion is, the serious point that it makes has in fact been demonstrated to be the basis for animal locomotion in many different species, from humans to birds, bees, and even bats (who use an echolocation variant of the optical flow).[5]

The perspective flow of the optic array thus offers rich information to animals who need to get around in the environment. Aspects of the flow specify such important environmental facts as where one is heading and how soon one will get there (or, conversely, how fast that thing over there is going to get here and collide with me!).

Optical information about *what* those objects are is not

contained in the flow field's poles and lines of longitude, but it is contained internally within the optic flow, especially in patterns of what Gibson called *occlusion*. Imagine once again that you are in the car. Now notice that the guardrails stand between you and a rocky field. As you whiz past, each guardrail appears to move in front of a specific region of the rocky field and then pass by, revealing the region, after which it is temporarily concealed by the next guardrail, and so on. This is the occlusion of further surfaces by a nearer surface. It resembles what painters call interposition (when one image in a picture blocks out or seems to be on top of a second image), except that it is an event, something that happens in the case of a moving observer rather than a static picture. Being an event, occlusion has a beginning (when the *leading edge* of the nearer surface starts to hide the farther surface), a middle (as the nearer surface appears to move over the further one), and an end (when the background surface is once again completely visible, emerging from the *trailing edge* of the nearer surface). Note that occlusion is also a law of nature, but a law dependent upon a subject, upon observation: the region of background that is occluded for you is not what is occluded for me, for I have a different viewpoint.

Information from occlusion is continually available because we live in a cluttered environment, and when animals observe their environment they are almost continually in motion, or getting ready to move—except for unusual cases like watching television. Occlusion is important because it specifies what is nearer or farther from me, and it specifies the shapes of things, by providing information about the *edges* of objects and their *orientation*. When we cannot see the edge of an object, we often move around that object or turn it around in order to obtain better occlusion information about the edges and their orientation.

Occlusion also provides the basic information for what psychologists call the permanence of objects. An object is permanent if it looks the same after it comes out from behind an occluding surface as it did when it went behind the surface, as does the bird flying in and out of the branches of a tree. Or, for that matter, as does the tree when we turn away from it and then look back to it. In contrast, the glint of light on the surface of a car window does not remain unchanged before and after the car enters a tunnel. And the shape of a puff of smoke changes as it moves through the branches of a tree. If an object is not so kind as to move by itself, however, you must look around so as to create the patterns of occlusion necessary to distinguish permanent from impermanent things.

As an observer moves through the environment, two special occluding edges move with her. The first is her own self, especially her skull. As a human observer, she looks out past her nose and the orbits of her eyes, which occlude what passes behind the head as she turns and looks at things. To see whatever has passed out of sight behind her head, she has to rotate this special occluder so that the leading edge reveals (disoccludes) what she saw earlier, and the trailing edge conceals (occludes) what she was just looking at. The second occluding edge that is intimately tied to our mobility is the local environment or vista. As one moves forward in a cluttered environment, what was concealed behind the far edges of the field of view is slowly revealed. As I move down the block and around the corner, I gradually come to see the next street. As I move through the meadow I gradually see what is on the other side. In general, as I move I open up the vistas in front of me and close down those behind me. And, once again, this pattern is reversible.

As Gibson noted in 1969, the information made available by optical occlusion can resolve some long-standing metaphysical debates.[6] How do I know whether that thing over there is a real object or something in a dream or a hallucination? Easy. I look at it and see whether it is moving. If it is, does it occlude and disocclude the background systematically, as a solid, opaque object should do? If it is not moving, I can move toward it and test whether it occludes the background appropriately as a function of my movement. Smoke, mirror images, holographic images, and hallucinations all fail this simple test. Even mirages fail this test, although perhaps the thirsty traveler would rather not notice that they have no location on the ground but always hover at a fixed distance away, no matter how much he moves. Indeed, the only way Descartes's evil demon could make a dream or a hallucination mimic patterns of occlusion would be to make it move (or not) in carefully timed coordination with each and every movement I use to inspect it. Often we do not want to experience dreams and hallucinations as we do the ordinary world, and therefore we do not pay attention to these subtle differences. Why ruin the fun? But this lack of *interest* in separating illusion from reality is not the same as a lack of *ability*.

Many readers may balk at such a "simple" solution to the deep philosophical problem of distinguishing illusion from reality. But why should the solution to this problem not be simple? (And, like all classical solutions, this one seems simple now that it is stated—but it took approximately three centuries to work out that simple solution.) The question asked by countless philosophers has been, "How can I tell whether a thing is something in a dream, a hallucination, or a real object?" The answer—examine its pattern of occlusion—provides a concise and *complete* answer to the question. True, an observer might not wish to test the question or perhaps not be able to test it at that time, but these are separate matters.[7] Could one dream that one was engaged in such a test of occlusion? Perhaps, but careful scrutiny will quickly reveal the dream or prove the reality. Occlusion is a relatively simple fact of primary experience that enables us to test whether experienced objects are real. As Gibson put it, the ecological analysis of experience gives us "new reasons for realism."[8]

Those who remain skeptical of the power of occlusion to specify reality would do well to ponder two more cases. These are the only cases where a mobile observer looking around *cannot cause changes* in occlusion patterns, and therefore the occlusion cannot help us distinguish reality from dream. No matter how much I try, I cannot see what is inside my head. Every way I move, I see only whatever part of the background environment is revealed or concealed by my turning head. My head itself is a large, mobile, occluded region in my field of view (for humans, it is approximately a hemisphere) that always hides behind the occluding edges at the orbits of my eyes. Similarly, what lies on the other side of and is occluded by the sky cannot be made visible by any terrestrial action I take.

In our ecologically rooted primary experience, then, there are only two things that stay persistently invisible despite our exploratory efforts: the insides of our skulls and the other side of the sky. With regard to these we cannot distinguish dream from reality within experience because the ordinary method of using occlusion to make this distinction is unavailable. It is particularly striking that two of the most ancient mysteries of human life, the nature of the soul and the idea of heaven, are directly related to the law of occlusion.

Occlusion is thus one of the most important ways to keep in touch with the world around us. Patterns of occlusion and disocclusion help us to distinguish objects from shadows, to see where we are, and to see where we are going. It is a part of firsthand experience, something all children learn for themselves, with little help from adults or school (with little recourse to secondhand experience). Of course, other perceptual capacities beyond those involved in occlusion and vision also contribute to helping us discover our place in the world. Primary, "uneducated" experience gives us this sense of ourselves and of our path through life, and in so doing brings us into meaningful contact with other people; in the course of that contact, we begin to acquire information from others, to build up our secondhand experience. Through this secondhand experience we learn about both the world outside our immediate sphere and the intricacies of human interaction. Yet even the most rarefied secondhand experience has roots in the rich and fertile soil of primary experience, of each individual's awareness of his or her place in the world and path through it.

### OPENING UP TO THE WORLD

Up to this point I have been focusing on firsthand experience, what we can observe directly of our surroundings. Firsthand experience seems easy: you just have to look (listen, feel, taste, smell)! But appearances can be deceiving, and much of what we think of as firsthand experience may actually emerge from a social context. We humans do not usually grow up in isolation. We are, in fact, mighty close to helpless at birth, and we spend much of our first two years learning how to act in and experience our worlds.[9]

Modern studies of human infants have revealed that, despite babies' helplessness, they are born with fairly sophisticated perceptual skills. And, interestingly, these perceptual skills are tied to interaction and sociality. Newborn babies are especially interested in human faces and voices and are able to detect patterns in the flow of facial and vocal expression. Being able to detect patterns, however—and even being able to respond to them—is not the same as experiencing the meanings of human actions. Probably newborns are born with the capacity to apprehend at least some important meanings, such as the difference between happy and sad faces, but equally probably most meaningful experience emerges from a long process of learning and apprenticeship.

Here we can detail three key elements in the development of experience: the ability to understand *animacy* (the distinction between living and dead things), *causality* (how one event leads to another), and *intention* (the role of specific goals in guiding behavior). These all rest on both the infant's firsthand ability to detect patterns in the events around her and her sensitivity to guidance from others—which ultimately becomes secondhand experience. Games like "peek-a-boo" and "bouncy-bouncy-oops!" are caregivers' ways of giving babies information about these three key features of experience. Once infants gain some mobility and autonomy (through sitting and crawling) they begin to acknowledge the rules of games, thus showing sensitivity to social meanings. A ten-month-old, for example, may take the hand of a caregiver and "make it" do the next step in a game. This is the beginning—crude and nonspecific as it may be—of true shared awareness, in which two people are doing the same thing and acknowledging that fact. Much still has to happen for the child's interactive abilities to flourish and mature, but it is at this juncture that she is in some real sense sharing experiences with others, and her experience is capable of growing in the social context.

Before she is a year old, then, a baby has discovered how to do what philosophers and social theorists for the past three centuries have declared to be impossible: share her experience with others without the use of language. This is because her sharing and experience are based on information, not on subjective, Cartesian ideas. She is not receiving ideas from others, nor is she transmitting ideas to them. Her caregivers are making information available to her, some of which she is capable of understanding; and she is making information available to them, some of which they are capable of understanding. They are making her aware of things and she is beginning to be able to make them aware of things. Although awareness is an achievement of individuals, it is not a subjective process, and it tends to be guided by others as well as by oneself.

The toddler who has just learned how to walk thus moves about in a *populated* environment. If she starts to go some place or do something forbidden by her caregiver, she may be stopped. She is learning slowly—much too slowly, as far as most caregivers are concerned—that not everybody shares her intentions. At the same time she is exploring objects and her powers to cause changes in them: to pick them up, to kick, poke, pinch, bite, pat them. In so doing, she receives rich arrays of ecological information—auditory, tactile, and chemical (taste and smell) as well as visual—all the while having certain ideas and actions encouraged and others discouraged. This is how toddlers become socialized, through a seamless mixture of firsthand and secondhand experience.

We are surrounded by information. I have described some of the information we use to see our place in the world, but there is also a great deal of information in the sounds, smells, and feels of our surroundings. While not the cause of experience, this information is the basis for it. Without it we can have no specific awareness of our surroundings.

One is rarely aware of information as such; typically, one responds to what the information specifies—some fact of the environment. This is especially obvious in the case of touch. As we feel things, we rarely notice the changing patterns of deformation of our skin or changes in position of our skeleton, but we almost always perceive something about the object. As we run our fingers over a surface, we notice its roughness or smoothness, not the bumps on our fingers. As we heft a package to feel what is in it, we do not notice the weight and pressure on our palms, but we do notice the distribution of weight and material in the package (did something move in there?).

In standard Western psychology and philosophy these things, which are typically *outside* our experience, are raised to the status of *causes* of experience. (Here again is the causal theory of perception that I criticized in Chapters 1 and 2.) Traditional theory tells us that unconsciously we register the pressures on our skin, and from these sensations of pressure we determine what caused them. Perception thus becomes a process of inferring what caused our (unconscious) sensations.

An information-based theory of perception puts these

sensations in their proper place, not as causes of perception but as *side-effects,* which can be noticed under special conditions. While eating your favorite food you can think about the sensations of pressure and resistance in your mouth as well as the isolated sensations of sweet, salty, or bitter on your tongue, but it takes a special effort to do so instead of simply savoring the food's taste and texture—and you might bite your tongue in the process. While caressing a lover you can notice the pressure on your own skin (and sometimes doing so is quite desirable), but as often as not you are attempting to gauge the needs, intentions, and movements of your partner.

Perceptual experience is determined by information but not caused by it. What the information specifies is what one perceives (what philosophers call the content of the perception): Is the food gristly or gelatinous? Is the skin supple or flabby? In order to perceive these things an observer has to explore: to look and to listen, to feel and to savor. We must learn how to investigate, just as doctors have to learn how to percuss and palpate our abdomens to perceive the state of our lungs and livers. And we have to learn how to attend to subtleties in the information we explore: an experienced cook can quickly tell whether the omelet is cooked enough to be folded, but this important information may escape the novice.

Experience is thus an activity embedded in a potentially lifelong process of learning, just as Dewey suggested. Whereas traditional theories treat experience as the product of a mental act—a judgment based on inferences—the information-based theory treats it as a potential achievement. To perceive something is to enter into a rapport with it as a meaningful object, place, or event. Perception in this sense is not merely mental; it is an act that best serves to unify mind and body; it is an achievement of the whole person who is looking, listening, scrutinizing, and discerning. We may start out with poor and disordered experience but come to develop an acute awareness of many things.

When a child learns to ride a bike, for example, she cannot feel the difference between being balanced and not. Her experience is disordered. Yet through practice and encouragement her sense of balance gradually becomes educated to this new task, and off she goes.

The standard Western, sensation-based theory of perception makes knowledge of the world hypothetical, analogous to scientific hypothesis, whereas information-based theory makes knowledge of the world partial, analogous to the acquisition of a skill. Most children fall any number of times before they master the art of riding a bicycle. Does this mean that their perception of balance and of the road is hypothetical and uncertain, as Descartes and his followers insist? I think not. At first the child's perception of balance is poor, but then it improves. She is not testing hypotheses about the nature of reality but learning through available information how to control her actions. The assumption of traditional Western thought is that truth and knowledge need to be absolute in order to be accounted truth and knowledge. This is a direct consequence of Descartes's myth of the evil demon. But perception in the ecological sense is true without being perfect or absolute. I can guide my actions in the world without knowing (or even claiming to know) everything about my surroundings. I may not be able to give an exhaustive report on the nature of my world, but I can walk around without falling or bumping into things—and, for that matter, I can do and understand quite a bit more as well. Even more important, if I pay attention, I can learn to do new things: I can improve my ability to perceive events and to control my activities.

## WHY POSTMODERNISTS REVEL IN BEING COUCH POTATOES

From an ecological perspective, experience is thus not so much something one has as it is a process of learning in which one engages. The fruits of experience are not stores of ideas but knowledge, especially know-how. An experienced person has more know-how than an inexperienced one, and this applies as much to secondhand experience and interpersonal activities as it does to the skills acquired through firsthand experience. Perceptual learning, as Gibson liked to say, occurs primarily outside of school—because this kind of learning can and should accompany us in everything we do. But our postmodern world seems bent on depriving us of opportunities for enriching our experience.

All animals have some ability to observe their environment, and to take from it whatever knowledge they need to perform their daily activities. Most birds and mammals make as much use of perspective-flow patterns as you or I. What makes human beings unique is the level to which we have developed our experiential skills with respect to objects, materials, and other people. Human survival has, until recently, depended upon the ability of individuals to learn to experience the properties of soils, wood, stone, minerals, and plants and to make our lives by means of these skills. Human survival has also depended on our skill at experiencing what others are thinking and feeling and shaping our actions to fit this knowledge, whether in ordinary social interactions or in more special cases of ritual, nurture, dance, or sex.

For increasing numbers of people, these basic patterns of human life are no longer operative. After more than a century of industrialization, Adam Smith's hyperdivision of labor has become common to workplaces around the globe. Each of us knows a great deal about our own tiny bailiwick (the making of pins, perhaps, to use Smith's example) and far too little about anything else. Moreover, the rules and regulations of a typical workplace actively discourage our attempts to learn about the entire work process or to share work with our colleagues and friends. Hannah Arendt complained about much of this decades ago in *The Human Condition* (1958). The only thing that has changed since then is that managers have found it possible to use computerization and information technology to extend this division of labor into service industries, which had previously been shielded from extensive segregation.

History does not reverse itself, and we as a society shall not return to the practices of Arendt's time or before; we will certainly not return to a preindustrial society. Nevertheless, if we are to go forward in a positive direction, we must learn from the changes our society has made; we must try to learn from them what things of value have been lost and seek ways to regain them. The defeatist use of the phrase "That's progress" to stifle debate about the value of experience in an increasingly technologized world is, in effect, a capitulation to the managerial perspective. Throughout this book I have been trying to show that there is a more human perspective from which to view these changes. We need to learn the lessons of this more human perspective before the cumulative effects of the changes overwhelm us.

What have especially changed for the worse since Arendt wrote are not only our workplaces and our jobs but our home life and our leisure. We don't just learn at work or in school, thank goodness. The things we do on our own—hiking, crafts, hobbies, just sitting and thinking—also help us learn. And the traditional activities of families—games, crafts, collective chores, and the like—serve the same purpose. Indeed, these informal and homely pursuits are perhaps the best ways of encouraging us to learn from our environment. And we have all but stopped doing any of them because of a relatively recent phenomenon, the culture of television.

Even television's critics have a hard time coming to grips with the full scope and power of its influence. Criticisms of the content of television shows, for example, however justified, address only one aspect of television's force. (Again, I am speaking of the cultural reality of television—its technics, not merely its technology.) Scores of studies in the past few decades confirm what we can easily observe for ourselves: in most American households, at least one television is turned on at least half the time anyone is present. (Whether anyone is actually watching the television is much harder to determine.) As a social phenomenon this is absolutely unprecedented in the history of the world. Even in the most devout times, few people spent as much as a tenth of their waking hours in prayer, much less a quarter or more. Sociologists today would consider people who went to church for half as long as most people watch television obsessively religious. In the history of the world I can think of only one other activity that has been pursued by such a high percentage of the population for so many hours in the day: food production. And even then, solely in preindustrial societies. The only activity that comes close to being as extensive as television viewing nowadays is work—but *work* covers so many different kinds of activities for different people that it is not really comparable to the unanimity with which we watch television.

Because television pervades modern culture, it is important to note its good aspects as well as its bad. With the advent of modern satellite technology, television serves as a purveyor of mass-produced information and a global synthesizer of that information. It is a cheap and efficient way to disseminate information worldwide. If that were all television was—if it were just a technological instrument—it would be a boon to humankind.

But for a variety of reasons, television has become much more than a source of information; it is the center of modern home life, the altar around which multitudes of lives revolve. An activity as pervasive as television viewing leaves little time for other activities. Its ubiquity thus poses a serious threat to opportunities for experiential learning in one of the most important centers for such learning: the home. Now people look at television; they no longer look at things for themselves. And given the constraints of modern schools and workplaces, we need all the outside opportunities for experience we can get.

All secondhand information is limited because it is necessarily selected. Even the most informative picture, videotape, or interactive CD-ROM cannot help us see things for ourselves. On a television or video screen, scrutiny of the physical world is replaced by passive regard of an image, varied only by choices from a menu or, in the somewhat misleading current metaphor, channel surfing. All criticism of the content of television is therefore moot. Even if television shows were consistently first-rate, watching television would still inhibit the development of perceptual learning, which would still be something to worry about.

Reading cookbooks is not the same as cooking, and seeing even the greatest chef in the world make a soufflé on a CD-ROM will not replace the experience of trying to make a soufflé yourself. And I don't know about you, but when I elect to undergo surgery, I should prefer a surgeon who has had at least a little firsthand experience to one who has spent years studying surgery on a CD-ROM.

Boosters of television and information technology assume that the viewer is going to take this secondhand information and integrate it into direct experience. The surgeon who is trained on television, we are assured, will also receive hands-on experience. But who will find the time and money to ensure that this happens, when so much of both are thrown away on the technology? Why not emphasize from the beginning that primary experience must be the basis for learning and that it is a source that can be supplemented, when reasonably called for, by secondhand information?

The argument that secondhand education will always be integrated with firsthand learning is misleading in two ways. First, our cultural experience confirms that unless we are careful, television viewing expands to fill the available time. Second, many of the things we need in order to integrate the experience we get from television with firsthand experience are hard to come by. When I was growing up I never had half the things I needed to do what Mr. Wizard did on television. And what person, or even school, has everything necessary to replicate some of the phenomena shown on, say, *Nova?* I remind the reader that in the same year that as a society Americans spent hundreds of billions of dollars on an information superhighway it was discovered that approximately one-third of our school buildings were substandard or even dangerous. Perhaps a hundred million dollars (approximately one-thousandth of what is needed) will be delegated to solve this problem, but there are signs that the money will not become available because of a widely perceived need for fiscal austerity.[10] As a society we have been fiscally austere with everything pertaining to hands-on experience, but we have been lavish with money and resources for improving secondhand experience.

### TELEVISION AND THE SEGMENTATION OF IMAGES

More speculatively, there is one more area for concern about the hegemony of television in our cultural life. This concern stems from what some postmodernists think is the best thing about television: the way it uses montage.[11] Television, video, and computer displays offer, as I have been emphasizing, selected information, and the process of selection raises important questions about modes of organization and presentation of information. Increasingly, these media offer their information through the use of montage, even what might be called multilevel montage. In montage, an event is filmed and recorded from several points of view, then the various linear sequences are chopped into fragments and made into a larger set from which a representation of the event is selected. In multilevel montage, the sound as well as the image is given this treatment, and, typically, several subsidiary or secondary events and their representations are also brought into the mix.

This is great fun and it makes for fast-moving, snappy commercials and music videos. Assuming for the sake of the argument that the caliber of these montages is excellent, the fact remains that montage by definition replaces the causal structure of real experience with narrative structure(s) and voice(s). (This is precisely why it is so acclaimed as a new art form.) Yet, great art as it might be—indeed, precisely because it is artistic—montage cannot substitute for ordinary experience. In every human skill much of what we learn is how to make things happen through certain specific steps, whether we are planting seeds, throwing a pot, making a gourmet dinner, or running a scientific experiment. If all our perceptual learning were based on montage, we would not be prepared for any of these homely endeavors, any more than the learning of these skills would prepare us to enjoy the latest music video. Let us not eliminate montage from its rightful place in the world, but let us at the same time be careful to help facilitate the attentive experiencing of complex events and relationships in the world of everyday life.

In addition, one of the most important kinds of everyday skill that we all need to acquire is the complex of movements involved in scrutiny. In order to carefully observe objects and events for oneself one has to have some understanding of events in general and their causal, sequential structure. The homesteader knows how to look for wind, water, sun, and drainage patterns, anticipating the seasonal events that will affect his or her home. The potter knows what will happen to clays and glazes under many different conditions of use. The nurse understands bodily functions and thus can see what is happening to his patient. Anyone with any ability to look for himself knows how to study even novel situations to find the patterns by which they are unfolding. From this kind of perceptual learning we gain our experience of being a part of the flow of life. The experience of being a part of something is especially relevant to social encounters, which are the most important everyday events, and it is this kind of experience that even the best video montages cannot offer.

The advent of montage in film and television has helped to liberate self-styled postmodern thinkers from some of the intellectual shackles of Western thought. A film can be about an event without copying that event. No one can actually view a baseball game from behind the catcher, in center field, and just above the dugouts simultaneously; practically, we can't move that quickly from one vantage point to another. But many of us have happily watched television montages of games from just those perspectives. Traditional, sensation-based theories of perception forced us to think of experience as being separated from the world, as a hypothetical model or representation of reality. In turn, this concept of experience has fit in all too nicely with our overall cultural drift away from the everyday. Our intellectual trends have exalted specialization and abstraction over common sense and hands-on know-how. At the same time, our social trends have increasingly marginalized the value of skilled craft labor. Now, in a final irony, postmodernists like Rorty reject the whole Cartesian worldview and insist that the philosophical ideals of truth and representation are myths. Montage teaches that representations cannot and need not truly resemble reality. Hence, none of us really know the world we inhabit.

The postmodernists are right about everything except their conclusion. Representations cannot be true. But the demise of representationalism does not undermine truth or the claim that we each genuinely experience our surroundings. Neither the representationalists nor the postmodernists have any concept of information or of exploratory activity, and therefore they have no understanding of how perception works. Postmodernists know, from their own experience, how valuable experience can be. Yet they have made no place for it in their theories. For all these theorists, what I call firsthand experience simply does not exist. The reason our intellectuals and educators do not defend firsthand experience from the widespread assaults on it in our culture is that they choose to be blind to its importance. Neither philosophers nor psychologists appreciate any kind of perceptual learning, not even the simple perceptual learning and the shared

awareness available to one-year-olds. Both representationalists and anti-representationalists have insisted that truth in perception must resemble accuracy of representation. But just as representations are rarely copies of the scene represented, neither is first-hand experience a copy of the world. This does not mean that there is no world or that there is no truth. It means that the perceptual theories on which both modernists and postmodernists have relied are wrong.

Finding truth in perception is not like matching a model to what it models. Nor is it a solitary or subjective process. Finding truth in perception is more like planing an edge of a piece of wood until it is "true" and will therefore make a good join. One has to hunt for relevant information and then use it. This not only takes work, it often takes time and learning. Notice that perception can be true even when a mistake is made. I can see and believe that the edge will be true, but I can be wrong. I can see and believe that a rock will come out of the ground easily only to find, after a little digging with my mattock, that it is a concealed boulder and will take an hour to dislodge. Experience consists of these kinds of truths and falsities—to adapt a metaphor of William James's, these are the perches on which our experience rests momentarily as it wings along.

Unlike the subjective ideas of standard theories, information-based truths (or falsities) are not private. When we are working together building a cabinet, you and I may disagree on how true the edge is—and if the join proves poor, one of us may well say "I told you so!" Because information is in the environment it can be shared, and we often learn best and have the richest experience when we have a guide. Our guide does not transmit ideas to us, nor does she impose certain ways of thinking upon us. A good mentor helps us to learn things for ourselves, to learn to attend to the available information. ("Look, when you hold it like this, you can see how the edge is slightly bowed in the middle.") Shared experience is educational because a mentor can help guide us to information we might not otherwise use or might use wrongly. Without a mentor we could be wrong and not know why, or we could be right, but still not know why.

In the modern Western view of experience the sharing of ideas and experiences is something like sharing secrets. Here is where the inherent paranoia of Western philosophy comes out: How can we know the mind of another person? How can we know that the whole secret has been shared? Obviously, we can't. In the ecological view, sharing experience is like sharing an activity, either among equals or in some kind of master-apprentice relationship. We may do everything together, or we may divide up the responsibility. But however we divide things up, we each contribute part of the whole. It is not a matter of my having a representation that *matches* yours but rather of my experience (and actions) *fitting in* with yours. If the two activities do not mesh, then we are not sharing. Think of trying to get a fifteen-month-old to help clean up after a bath. While you are organizing and tidying, the child is probably pouring water on the floor and exploring the puddle. The two of you are sharing the place but not the activity, nor the experience. On the other hand, sharing a place is not a trivial thing, and the child will, we hope, come to learn how to share the activity and experience in time.

Simple as this example and the concept of sharing-as-fitting are, the idea has profound implications. Modernists and postmodernists alike conceive of community as based on *matching* ideas or ideals. In this view, when I am said to be in agreement with you, it is on the basis not of shared work or shared experience but of shared ideas—of making our representations of reality match. Developing this notion, Enlightenment modernists sought a universal ideal that could be matched by all people (liberty, equality, fraternity, human rights, whatever). Postmodernists like Rorty disparage this search, saying that one idea cannot suit everyone; matching ideals can be found only for relatively small groups. Perhaps so, but if matched ideals are not the

basis of community, then both the universalizability of ideals and its alleged failure are *irrelevant* to the question of how we can share our experiences.

What we need—and in my opinion need pretty desperately—is for people to learn how to fit and work together. This will happen when, as a society, we make an effort to encourage both firsthand experience and the sharing of that experience in schools, workplaces, and homes. The task is simple, inexpensive (although it demands the expenditure of human time and effort), and adaptable. How long can we bemoan the breakdown in civility and complain about the decline of everything from morals to book-learning before we realize that these things cannot be force-fed to people like a pill or impressed on their senses like a television commercial? People must develop these experiential skills by themselves and learn them slowly, over the course of many experiences. Neither the modernist emphasis on "universal" standards nor the postmodernist call for separate cultures offers a solution as practicable as my emphasis on experience, care, and concern.

Echoing Dewey, I assert that communities are made by activities that broaden and deepen real sharing. Real sharing is not the matching of ideals—whether spontaneous, forced, coaxed, or inculcated. Real sharing is acting and experiencing together. This is the opposite of the machining process. There, people's experiences are made to fit into preexisting ideas: a boss's flow chart for a workplace or a rigid educator's micromanaged curriculum. But in a real community of people who are trying to join their actions and experiences one sees shared exploration and performance, the attempts to locate meaning and values that can be made to *work together*. Note that working together does not mean that the values match. A nurse can prefer to comfort the patient as a whole person, while the surgeon may prefer to help the patient by operating on the diseased part, yet nurses and surgeons can and do work together. Further, one sees that the inarticulate basis of sharing in firsthand experience is typically overlaid with explicit information sharing (secondhand experience)—from simple things like the command to "look at that" to the complex instructions needed to teach the new nurse the correct order in which to hand instruments to the surgeon (which the experienced nurse, in turn, teaches the greenhorn surgeon).

Even this cursory review of an alternative theory of experience—the ecological approach—helps us to see just how far off track Descartes and his followers have pushed us. Western philosophers and psychologists alike have conceptualized experience as being comprised of two separate mechanisms embedded within a communication system—the body signaling the mind. These theorists see our contact with the world as physical and therefore meaningless until it is interpreted by the mind, and they treat our contact with other people as a matching of internal mental interpretations of bodily signals. Ironically, although this view of experience corresponds poorly with how most people have grown up and learned about the world, it increasingly seems to correspond to how our children will grow and learn—because we are *making* our schools and workplaces into little Cartesian prisons.

But experience can be looked on as something intrinsic to life, activities we can carry out by ourselves or in community with others. Firsthand experience can be enhanced and enriched by secondhand—if the people involved know how to share experience and to make that sharing their goal. So how do we motivate people to stop being wooden, to come alive, to learn to thrive in their experience, and, ultimately, to learn how to share their experience with others?

# SIX  Experience and Love of Life

Modern Western theories of experience are based on sensation, not information. Because of this they make no distinction between first- and secondhand experience, nor do they help us understand what makes experience good or bad, nor do they help us understand how experience can motivate people to act.

If all experience is composed of subjective sensations, then we never experience our surroundings directly—like Descartes, we can at best only infer what goes on around us. Learning about the world becomes akin to having one part of ourselves tell another part what is going on—when neither part has genuine access to the situation.[1] Any evaluation of experience is thus hamstrung, to say the least. In spite of the twists and turns of various theorists, one is ultimately reduced to a bastardization of Duke Ellington's philosophy of music. Instead of his wise "If it sounds good, it is good," these theorists give us the inane "If it seems good, it is good." If our direct awareness is always limited to the seemings of internal sensations—to the subjective sensations caused by the blowing of instruments into the air, not the music itself—then no matter how we squirm intellectually, our only criteria for evaluating experience as good or bad will be internal feelings, not the actual sound of the band.

For centuries philosophers have constructed elaborate houses of cards to obscure the weakness of the sensory foundations of their theories of value. They have offered many criteria for value and truth: consistency, simplicity, elegance, utility, correspondence to scientific facts or to metaphysical essences—but in the final analysis, Western theorists of experience have found themselves forced to offer a single test for all these apparently different criteria concerning the value of experience: Is this a sensory experience that seems good to the philosopher? Although different thinkers appear to prefer different criteria, such as simplicity or facticity, elegance or logical structure, none have been able to break out of the solipsistic circle so as to test experience against something other than their internal feelings. No wonder mainstream Western philosophy so disdains common experience. But most sensible individuals are just plain unwilling to restrict their definitions of good and evil to subjective feelings and would tell these philosophers where to get off.

Without an adequate theory of perception, no one has been able to offer a coherent intellectual response to this solipsistic account of value, which is what makes Gibson's work so important. Once we realize that it is possible *within* experience to distinguish reality from dream, we can get on with the business of understanding what makes experience important, its connection to motivation and action. As it turns out, the widespread subjective view of experience has led to an unacceptably reductionist account of motivation, which must also be revamped in the light of ecological psychology.

WHY WE DO WHAT WE DO

We all have favorite activities. Some people enjoy sports, others like playing music, some like both. Some people—not ourselves, of course—are driven and obsessed by incomprehensible needs. What does she get out of bungee jumping? How can he want to go hunting every weekend? What do they see in each other? Experience tells us that objectives and goals have different amounts of force for different people: we can see for ourselves that for some, bungee jumping is well-nigh irresistible, for others, well-nigh unfathomable.

The modern Western theory of experience, however, implies that our common view of this motivating force "must be" an illusion. If there is no such thing as bungee jumping—at least, if your subjective idea of bungee jumping and mine are completely different, and if neither of us experiences the real thing but only our internal feelings—then it cannot be bungee jumping as such that motivates or frightens us. No, it "must be" some internal state that does so.

There are as many philosophical and psychological theories of motivation as there are theories of value. But in order to conform with the basic anti-experiential presuppositions of Western philosophy, each of these theories winds up reducing motivation to an internal state or feeling. Some of the same ideas as are found in theories of truth also show up in theories of motivation: elegance, simplicity, or intensity are said to be features of feelings that motivate. But they ultimately come down to this formulation: what motivates us is a subjective state that causes positive feelings; what turns us off is a subjective state that causes negative feelings.

This reductionist account of motivation cannot withstand close scrutiny. We often find ourselves motivated to do things we clearly do not enjoy. Many a parent has wearily cleaned up vomit and diarrhea—and a few have even jumped into icy water to save their child—but it is difficult to believe that any of them enjoyed the associated subjective states. The standard theorist counters that these parents were motivated by other ideas and feelings in such cases, which took precedence over the subjective state of the moment (in other words, feeling good about helping your child allows you to ignore your internal discomfort or fear). Yet, at some point, even these variants of the theory break down, becoming little more than disguises for saying "I felt like doing x because I did not feel like doing x." The novice's first cigarette or first hit of heroin is a case in point. In both cases the average newcomer to the drugs becomes ill, but for some that is the point of the exercise and the motivation to return to the action is heightened. A theory that states that we are motivated to do those things that feel good, but then adds, "sometimes making ourselves feel bad is what makes us feel good," cannot be an acceptable theory. Common sense allows that motives may conflict: I might hate to get cold and wet but value my child's life more than my comfort. Yet under the subjectivist criteria of value emphasized in standard theories, this conflict must be reduced to the relative intensities of two subjective states, not the relative merits of two courses of action.

There is a further problem with such reductionist accounts of motivation. In part because they "explain everything" they do not help us to differentiate among motives. In the end, all motivation is reduced to positive feelings, genetic fitness, self-aggrandizement, or whatever universal factor the theorist currently favors. From a perspective that takes experience seriously, this is unfortunate. Not only is sexual activity typically experienced as being different from the activity of eating or singing, but the pleasures involved in each kind of activity are easily distinguished, even by novices. Indeed, were it not for the blinders placed on us by an anti-experientialist worldview, our culture might actually engage in the interesting and important discussion of the virtues and vices of the various forms of pleasures.[2]

Freud recognized many of the problems inherent in standard theories of motivation. In his theory of motivation (*trieben,* often translated as "drives" but perhaps better rendered as "wishes"), he did not resolve these issues, but he did recognize

them.[3] Let us look at the serious limitations inherent in one of the most articulate theories of motivation offered within a Western modernist worldview.

Freud's analysis of motivation goes hand in hand with his account of how young children begin to realize their individuality and separateness from other people and things. What is striking about Freud's version of the story of childhood is how seamlessly it mixes traditional psychological concepts—of the kind criticized here—with a version of Socrates' myth of *eros* from Plato's *Symposium,* a book that hardly fits within the bounds of standard theories.[4]

Infant experience begins, according to Freud, with an "oceanic feeling." In this the child feels united with the world (or, better, it feels a vague unity that has not yet been divided into self and world). In some ways the feeling of unity is pleasurable and in others unpleasant, but all the feelings are internal and undifferentiated. Like Socrates, who claimed that love was a constant search for a distantly remembered wholeness, Freud bases his pleasure principle on the search in later life to recapture this feeling of unity from early experience: seeking pleasure is seeking to be whole, as one was in the past. And, as in other modern psychological theories, Freud defines pleasure as an internal state; pleasure is noncognitive, it is just a feeling, in itself it is not an awareness of something beyond that feeling.

The reality principle for Freud is completely different from the pleasure principle. It is based, as in the theories we have reviewed, on the various sensations caused within the self by external things. Through experience with these externally caused internal states, the ego discovers that it is not the whole universe and begins to form an image of the world as distinct from the self. The experience of the infant is dominated by eros—by pleasure in unity—but this is transformed, says Freud, into the experience of the adult, who faces up to realities. Hence, within the adult is a set of pleasure-driven feelings (the id), a set of internalized rules taken from society (the superego), and a mediator between these (the ego). This mediator constructs an individual's experience as a kind of balance between the pleasure and reality principles.[5]

Freud uses the following example of how this works. As infants, children may enjoy wallowing in and manipulating their own feces. Over time, however, the reality principle (with the help of the superego's conveyance of social norms) interferes in this simple pleasure—and the child's earlier feelings undergo a reversal. Now the child experiences feces as unpleasant and repulsive. Note that Freud is not saying that the child's *attitude* toward or judgment of feces has changed (as standard cognitivist theories claim) but rather that the *feelings* themselves have changed. For Freud, such reversals can occur because experience begins by being completely internal. Freud sees direct experience as experience of things in the world, rather than experience of subjective states. Only by constructing a kind of secondhand world do we begin to interpret reality, an interpretation that can alter our experience of our place within the world and thus alter our feelings. Eros, in short, cannot be cognitive.

Experience of the world (cognition) is always mediated by the reality principle, not the pleasure principle. The id lives in a dream world of feeling, but it is nevertheless the force behind all our motives. Hence, our motives at root are merely desires to have certain feelings (for example, to return to the oceanic feelings of early childhood); motives are *not* desires to stand in a particular relation to the world. At best our relations with the world are substitutes for the feelings to which they give rise. The feelings aroused by sexual intercourse, for example, are for Freud the paradigm of all love. Hence Freud argues that all nonsexual loves (filial, brotherly, comradely, parental) are inhibited in their true aim: the feelings associated with intercourse. Thus, Freud sees not a variety of pleasures or loves but a single kind of feeling in a variety of contexts.

If our drives were blind to the world and could sense

only internal feelings, we might well confuse friendship with inhibited lust—there would be nothing to distinguish one good feeling from another, and our ids might try to take each good feeling as far as they could. But our drives are not blind to the world. Our feelings are not separated from our appraisal of our place in the environment. Both Socrates and Freud were wrong: eros is not always a longing for a longlost, never-to-be-achieved unity. Eros inhabits all manner of primary experience: our joy in being in the midst of life is the essence of eros, although that joy can take an infinite number of forms. Sexual intercourse is one kind, but it is only one, and it is not the paradigm, for there are as many varieties of pleasure as there are pleasurable objects. Primary experience can and should be active, engaged, and alive; therefore, it also should lead to every kind of pleasure.

### EROTIC EXPERIENCE

One of the saddest aspects of both modernism and postmodernism is their reductionist view of the erotic, a view that derives from their inadequate analysis of motivation. Eros is widely reduced to the subjective side of orgasm, in both popular and intellectual culture. Even those postmoderns who find an erotics in many places seem obsessed with the feelings associated with intercourse. Freud's view of joy as essentially inhibited orgasm rules supreme.

I do not wish to denigrate sexuality, not even inhibited orgasm. Erasmus Darwin (Charles's grandfather) rightly said that sexuality is the crown of creation. But the anti-experiential worldview gives a highly distorted view of sexuality, missing out on the erotic aspects of everyday experience. In fact, it is difficult to talk about these aspects precisely because once the word *eros* is used readers make the false assumption that one is talking about orgasm. According to standard thinking, erotic feeling must be private and rooted in the subjective feelings associated with sexual congress.

If experience of the world is possible, and if motives are pegged to objects in experience, we can be motivated to seek out as many things as there are. (To use Freud's language against his own theory, we can have an indefinite number of autonomous drives or wishes.) Moreover, the positive or negative feelings that accompany our actions are part of experiencing the world, not isolated, interior states.

Hence, every object is potentially meaningful and a potential source of joy or sorrow. The infant's experience does not start out as subjective and driven by feeling, only to be forced into shape by a cruel real world or a crueler social world. Even infants experience some of the things around them. They appreciate their pleasures and pains not as subjective sensations but as part of their encounters with the world. They both discover the values of things ("Hey, this shiny thing swings when I slap it") and, through accrued experience, come to *imbue* things with meaning ("This is the teddy bear I always sleep with").

Socrates was right that eros is at heart a desire to unite with an object, but he was wrong to make this a spiritual uniting of soul and idea. And Freud was wrong to identify all nonsexual eros as a veiled substitute for the feelings of unity in sexual intercourse. The eros of everyday experience, the joy of lived experience, is simply the love of life, the pleasure of encounter and use. Eros is intrinsic to our encounters with objects and situations; it is neither a surrogate for anything else nor a subjective feeling. Because everyday experience is intrinsically full of feeling and based on a variety of motives—because it is *erotic,* if one can recapture the original meaning of the word—it is alive and can grow.

For anyone who routinely takes pleasure in doing things—cooking, gardening, sewing, building, music, sports—the need to emphasize that such pleasures are intrinsic to actions shows the hopelessness of standard psychology. These activities are not thwarted acts of intercourse. They are homely ways of being in touch with our surroundings and, as such, are pleasurable. When primary experience is part of daily life, joy is part of daily life as well.

The limited truth in Freud's account of child development lies in his emphasis on the growth from feeling to action. Babies have limited physical skills but remarkable powers of perception.[6] They attend to ever-increasing subtleties of events, both natural and social. And from an early age they show pleasure in both comprehension and control, even where their skills of experience and action are limited.

Under normal conditions of nurturance the caregiver recognizes and helps develop the baby's pleasure in comprehension and control through games of call and response, of echoed action, and, eventually, of rhythmic patterns. Later, caregiver and child will play games of attention and comprehension, which include nursery songs and rhymes. By the time a child can walk he has not only acquired some simple skills, he has in all likelihood become motivated toward certain things and away from others. As his capacity to act on his environment and on people evolves in the second and third year of life, he develops a unique collection of pleasures and, therefore, an increasingly distinctive set of experiences, joys, and sorrows. To be human is to experience one's place in the world as a special way of enjoying both the things and the people that surround us.

### NURTURING EXPERIENCE

I am not defending just any experience, although I am referring to everyday experience. Not all experience is good, and some can be downright bad. In his theory of education, John Dewey offers some useful pointers on distinguishing the two: "Any experience is mis-educative," he wrote, if it "has the effect of arresting or distorting the growth of further experience."[7] Some of the ways experience can be harmful include: desensitizing one to further experience; putting one in a rut (through overly automatized experiencing and action); promoting slackness by inhibiting further efforts that may be needed to benefit from experience; being too disconnected from other experience for it to be appropriately integrated into one's understanding or action.

Dewey's critique of education centered around these bad experiences because, Dewey claimed, modern schooling contains examples of such miseducative situations. And a similar critique could be made of modern workplaces. Much of what I described in Chapters 3 and 4 fits his pattern of miseducation. And, more generally, it seems clear that when primary experience is inhibited the most common effects are, indeed, desensitization, falling into a rut, slackness (especially of attention), and disconnectedness or scatteredness.

If the modern machining of the mind leads to these unhelpful experiences, how can we generate more fruitful experience? Dewey summarized his ideas about positive experience with the catchphrase: "The fine old saying 'A sound mind in a sound body' can and should be extended to read 'A sound human being in a sound human environment.' "[8] Let me try to flesh this out.

Let's begin with a reminder that experience as I define it here is always alive. Living things thrive only in certain conditions; denied those conditions, they grow poorly or not at all or even die. Experience, as we have seen, is a search for meanings in order to find and use the goods of the earth and the social world around us. Information is the first requirement for good experience, but it must come in conjunction with opportunities for exploration that lead to better contact with one's surroundings. Even babies (especially babies?) spend a considerable amount of time and effort looking at the world around them, feeling things in their mouths (and later in their hands), listening, tasting, and more.

Common sense, now backed up by research, tells us that babies who have little opportunity to explore their world do not develop as well as others. Indeed, we are now confident that brain development itself is in part a result of such exploratory activity. Note that this is not a matter of just "stimulating" the child.[9] Stimulation *without information,* without meaning, will do harm, not good, because the child's strategies of exploring and attending will ultimately be inhibited. There is also some evidence—far from conclusive—that infants will be most motivated to attend when they recognize that they are in control of access to the information. They would rather have information they can choose to access than a constant stream over which they have no control.[10]

By the time an infant becomes a toddler and is learning to talk the issue of control and autonomy becomes more crucial. I believe that the child's assertions of independence and difference (the two-year-old's "no") play a major role in helping it balance first- and secondhand experience.[11] At this stage in development, caregivers have to learn not only how to encourage exploration and activity in children but also how to let children do things for themselves. The need to experience and act for oneself is generally quite strong in people. If the child's social environment does not allow sufficient autonomous exploration or if it does not provide sufficient context for integrating the results of such exploration, the child's growth of experience will be retarded. It is becoming increasingly clear, for example, that television is a poor teacher of language skills in large part because there can be no dialogue with a television. Young children, of course, speak to their TVs, but television sets do not as yet answer back. Children with too much of this kind of experience tend to be delayed in a number of language skills.[12]

Once the child can balance its own interests, needs, and experiences with those of others, it is in a position to learn the skills of daily life. In most traditional, rural cultures, children as young as three may be found on the fringes of adult activities, beginning to learn for themselves what adult situations are like.[13]

We in the modern industrialized world have substituted an institution, schooling, for what heretofore was a grab bag of informal and formal modes of education.

Schooling can be a valuable provider of nurturing experience, if it is organized correctly. This requires not only that individuals balance first- and secondhand experiences but that communities do so. Dewey's stress on the importance of community derived from his analysis of what nurtures educative experience. A community of experiencers and agents represents a group of people who have joined together to do something. When kept relatively small such groups do not require the imposition of arbitrary authority to run smoothly. This is not to deny that conflict can occur in these groups. Of course it can, and it does. But such organic groups can often nurture experience successfully without requiring the invention of new—and to some degree arbitrary—rules and powers of authority, as do more formal institutions.[14]

In fact, one of Dewey's fundamental points is that to create and maintain a true democratic community, we need to educate people in the art of working together, so that they don't need arbitrary authority. Unlike most other critics of authoritarian education, Dewey was interested in freedom and autonomy for the pupil only as a means to an end: "Freedom from restrictions . . . is to be prized only as a means to a freedom which is power: power to frame purposes, to judge wisely, to evaluate desires by the consequences which will result from acting upon them." And, Dewey warned, "the mere removal of external control is no guarantee for the production of self-control."[15] Removing the conditions that nurture bad experience is by no means equivalent to producing good experiences. If, by some miracle, we eliminated all the bad schools in America this would by no means guarantee that the affected children would then begin to have valuable learning experiences. Far from it.

One of the weaknesses of Dewey's philosophy is that it can seem to emphasize process to the exclusion of product. Dewey can be read as celebrating exploration and growth to such a degree that he seems indifferent to the content of experience. Growth, he appears to be saying, is everything, and the goal of growth nothing. Indeed, some educational theorists have read Dewey in just this way, arguing that the content of education is unimportant; only the form of the educational process matters.[16]

Even Lewis Mumford, a social commentator who came to have much in common with Dewey, misread him in his influential *The Golden Day* (1924).[17] Mumford felt that Dewey's pragmatist philosophy, with its emphasis on process, was just a fancy way of endorsing a technocratic worldview: if a process can be made to run properly and smoothly, it is good, regardless of the product.

Such criticism is, I believe, unfair. But one can see how it arose, for Dewey was always vague about the content of experience. Even when defining good versus bad experience he tended to focus on process, not product. Regardless of the precise interpretation of Dewey's thought, however, the approach to these issues offered here is not, and should not be, indifferent to content. I start from the idea that good experience must facilitate perceptual learning and the growth of further experience. Overexposure to montage is bad not because of anything intrinsic to the montage experience but because it denies the viewer the opportunity to learn how to look at things for himself. Integrate the montage (or any video experience) with firsthand learning and the good aspects of both can be enhanced. In general, we need to promote the ability to experience the world. To do this we must recognize that a certain amount of hands-on, direct experience is crucial. Similarly, a certain amount of group engagement, of learning how to work on firsthand problems with others, is also crucial. These are experiences and activities that can be inculcated anywhere—school, work, home, community—but they are not currently receiving adequate attention.

The first tenet of the present approach is that experience is as much a function of the environment as of the self. For my experience to grow, it must come within a nurturing environment. In the case of the human environment, this means that respect for persons is a precondition for all growth of experience. But just this respect for ordinary, everyday people and their experience tends to be threatened by the changes we are undergoing in modern society.

Developing an argument drawn from poet Wendell Berry, Christopher Lasch suggests that respect for persons is central to promoting democracy. "The most important choice a democratic society has to make [is] whether to raise the general level of competence, energy, and devotion—'virtue,' as it was called in the older political tradition—or merely to promote a broader recruitment of elites."[18] Lasch argues that our society has opted for the second choice. We define success as upward mobility, not as the enhancement of each individual's experience to help to make us all worthy of respect. We look to elites and technocrats to solve social problems and doubt the ability of individuals and grass-roots organizations to do so. Yet it is obviously impossible for everyone to succeed in the climb for upward mobility. There must always be an immobile, or even downwardly mobile, group, even in the most affluent society; and one person's upward mobility is often balanced by another's downward slide. In contrast, good experience, which can engender respect for both oneself and others, can be spread universally.

We might thus redefine democracy, as Berry and Lasch suggest, and choose the first alternative: we can promote virtue instead of upward mobility and the dollar. To do this will require an emphasis on respect for ordinary experience and a willingness by intellectuals and educators to help give voice to people who might not otherwise have their voices heard in social discussions. And it will require encouraging us all to increase the time and effort we spend acquiring firsthand experience—both individually and collaboratively. Can love of life replace love of lucre? At the least we can try to orient our philosophy and our education in this new direction. Modern schooling typically consists of periods of book learning interspersed with occasional skills learning (physical education, music, shop). Almost never do we try to combine the two. Perhaps the best curricular insight Dewey ever had was how valuable it would be to integrate these related spheres of experience: to learn chemistry in the context of cooking, for example, or music in the context of mathematics.

The worst aspect of the modern degradation of experience is that it saps us of hope. As our opportunities and horizons become limited and constrained, we fail to see beyond the narrowest sphere of self-interest. Hence the modern paradox of every home having a television that carries information from all parts of the world about all sorts of people and more and more television viewers thinking and behaving selfishly. Similarly, as people become concerned with the state of public schooling around our country—a good sign of public interest and concern—they increasingly lament that the schools are hopeless and cannot be saved. Even many educators share this pessimism.

A society in which fewer and fewer people have control over their experience and fewer and fewer people learn how to take pleasure in expanding their horizons is ripe for nihilism. When people are motivated by a narrow range of private or subjective feelings, and when they don't know how to share the concerns and joys of their lives, their selfishness will inevitably increase. In such situations, it no longer makes sense to work with others; the smart move seems to be to look out for ourselves.

What is truly shocking about this widespread public nihilism is how off the mark it is. As a society, we could certainly organize and mobilize the resources for our purposes; after all, in the business sector, the annual expenditure on advertising and television commercials in the United States is approximately one *trillion* dollars. Combining every conceivable kind of expenditure for education, from the federal government to the local level, private and public, from daycare through graduate and professional schools, we spend perhaps 40 percent of that (approximately 400 billion dollars).[19] We have become the greatest salespeople of all time, and there is little doubt that we could sell ourselves on improving our lives—if we wanted to. Surely a society that has perfected the art of persuasion could do a bit more to encourage the growth of experience among the people in it. People doubt our ability to do so only because the attack on experience has shrunk our horizons. We cannot change this attitude of hopelessness or despair by argument. Instead, we need to figure out why hopelessness is on the increase, so that we can find a seed of hope to nurture here and now, not in some mythical utopia.

# SEVEN   Experience and the Birth of Hope

I have argued that a number of our society's psychosocial ills have a common root in our culture's disdain for primary experience. This disdain appears in both our theories and our practice. It is not the cause of these problems, nor is it the single most important cause of any given problem. But it is a pervasive contributor to them and one that, I believe, can be ameliorated or even rectified. Although these problems have been widely discussed elsewhere, the idea that they have a common source is novel. Because my argument has many strands, a brief summary is in order before I turn to some possible solutions.

On the theoretical side, I have argued that modern Western theories of experience exhibit contempt for primary human experience. Those theorists who have disagreed with the prevailing orthodoxy (Goethe, some of the existentialists) have not so much offered new theories to challenge our scientistic undermining of experience as they have simply protested against it. Even the work of James, Dewey, and Gibson praised here remains to be taken up and used in a coherent theory to redirect the way philosophers and scientists treat daily experience.

On the practical side, my arguments may be subject to debate precisely because antipathy to experience is only one factor among several important reasons that our schools, workplaces, and homes do not meet our psychological needs. I do not pretend to offer a complete account of these problems. Nevertheless, my analysis lets us go beyond existing ways of thinking about all of these problems, as in the following cases:

• We are witnessing reductions in the amount of meaningful work available to the average person, as well as reductions in opportunities for learning skills, whether at work or elsewhere. This trend has been described as a move away from a production-based to a consumer-based society, but if this were all there was to the change, it would not be so worrisome. The consumer-based culture in which we live thrives in part by depriving individuals of opportunities to gain direct experience. Moreover, information-based workplaces are currently forcing people to work long hours in confined settings. Opportunities for serious, protracted, firsthand learning could be part of our education, workplace, and leisure activities—but they are not.[1]

• Complaints about public education are so widespread nowadays that I hesitate to add my voice to what is often a fruitless chorus. Moreover, much of the debate seems to concern the inability of our current educational system to prepare students for their later working lives. But this argument assumes that preparation for work is the role of public education. I strongly disagree and instead endorse Adam Smith's still-radical concept that public education best serves us by giving children opportunities to develop experiential skills relevant to all aspects of their lives, not just to work. Education should be thought of as a process for integrating primary and secondary experience and should therefore be reconceptualized as a lifelong process that combines real-world problem solving with traditional school learning.

• It is not the technology of our era that is constraining the growth of experience in our society but the *technics,* the social arrangements that ruling elites attempt to foster, often through technological means. The widespread fear of primary experience—experience that might end in failure, or in unforeseen results—is a fear of a *necessary* part of everyday experience, a fear that has been inculcated in us solely in order to make life easier for machines. This has resulted in a form of stultifying social regimentation. What other culture limits the movements, thoughts, and speech of millions of people for the better part of the day, at least five days a week? If we want to promote experience we must change our technics, not our technology.

• Perhaps as a response to this stultifying work life, we have transformed our leisure by modern information technics. The widespread, intensive use of a single mode of "entertainment"—television—is historically unprecedented. This is problematic not because of the technology as such but because of its role in inhibiting the development of autonomous experience and perceptual learning.

• Taken together, these trends contribute to a lessening of both the opportunity for and the motivation underlying collaborative activity. As part of the regimentation of work and school we have come to accept a massive decrease in the opportunities for the spontaneous formation of groups to solve problems (or even simply to play). Combined with the psychological atomism engendered by watching too much television, this acceptance has led to a remarkable decline in human interaction. It is speculative, but hardly implausible, to see this decline as one of the causes of what has been called the increasing barbarism of daily life.

Each of these issues is a deep and serious problem, but I suggest that at least one factor—the degradation of everyday experience—underlies them all. Attempts to defend experience should thus have broad and positive social repercussions.

One of the great lessons of taking experience seriously is

that change must be sought on the basis of the actual conditions of the world. These are the only conditions that people find meaningful, and any changes that cannot be understood from an everyday perspective are unlikely to succeed. As William James discovered in his studies of religious conversion, we cannot suddenly alter all our habits and patterns of experience without making use of already developed and available patterns.[2] If we are to defend experience from the onslaughts of modernity, we can neither return to some mythical golden age nor expect a positive, postmodern approach to experience to arise on its own. We must instead work within existing patterns of experience. In the realm of experience there is no high tech and there are no quick fixes; there is only the slow, steady, sometimes joyful, sometimes painful growth of understanding.

### BROKERING EXPERIENCE

The historian of commercialism William Leach offers the most succinct description of "modern experience" I have ever seen: "The brokering style—repressing one's own convictions and withholding judgment in the interest of forging profitable relationships—is among the most modern of styles."[3] In other words, don't build on your own experience, and don't try to build upon what you have learned of the world, but follow what others are doing. In this one phrase, "the brokering style," Leach succeeds in capturing much of the dynamic of modern experience. First came the Cartesian separation of judgment from sense, which made judgment a private matter. What had been an objective claim—the making of judgments in social contexts—was increasingly seen as a subjective, private process.[4] Then the idea of being "judgmental" came to be seen as a negative thing, more or less equivalent to being biased (what used to be considered *pre*judgmental, which is to say, prejudiced). One of Leach's key themes is that this modern approach to judgment is a cultural construction. Where experience once was used to buttress a public position from which to judge others (and even oneself), it now functions largely on a private level.

Leach's concept of a brokering style also captures the invasion of so many sectors of modern experience by advertising. Modern advertising descends directly from the hucksterism P. T. Barnum made famous. But what was widely viewed as unabashed shysterism a century ago is intrinsic to modern enterprise; shysterism is nowadays accepted as part of life.[5] No one believes ads—certainly not the people who make them—but few people judge them on such mundane criteria as truth, reasonableness, or validity. To the extent that advertising permeates modern life (and with signs, billboards, print, radio, television, and telecommunications saturating our environment, *permeates* is perhaps too mild a word), our everyday experience is debased toward a brokering style.

Thanks to our trillion-dollar annual advertising economy, every child growing up in America is bombarded by advertisements. They have become a prominent part of our everyday experience. Children must learn to interpret these odd fragments of "information" as well as they can and, in addition, to interpret their social world when (if?) the people around them explain the way ads mislead and manipulate them. Children must thus come to grips with the idea that something they encounter many times every day was created precisely to mislead them. But after a while, the mental effort of dealing with ads becomes too much, and most of us simply succumb to them, treating them as ordinary (not suspicious) communication. The reality of coping with the ubiquitous falsehoods of advertisements is an important but unstudied part of the psychology of modern life.

Directly related to the experience of advertising are the problems of independent judgment in the workplace, where the much-vaunted freedoms of speech and thought on which the United States was founded have no place. To take an obvious example: employees dare not publicly challenge their company's advertising, even if that advertising is demonstrably false or misleading. Their judgment has become brokered; they cannot make use of the critical function of experience. But the paralysis of thought within the workplace goes much deeper. As we have seen, with the advent of information technology, many jobs process judgment out; these jobs are turning into prisons like the Chinese fortune-cookie prison. From nine to five independent thought and experience are increasingly seen as unhelpful "quirks" in the industrial-bureaucratic machine.

The brokering style has all but taken over our educational system, as well. School administrations broker the textbooks to be used in public schools, primarily because of well-organized religious groups. The fundamentalist view of the world, having lost out in serious intellectual debate within both history and science, has found that profit rules over truth. History or biology textbooks that reproduce in even the mildest form the *consensus* of scholarly opinion on their subjects may be boycotted. Therefore no such textbooks have been published in the past decade or two.[6] The goal of the boycotters is to see their own, ill-informed views presented as "equal" to far-better-substantiated theories. Publishers and educators alike have been suckered by this strategy, the publishers for profit, the educators in a misguided attempt to give "equal time" to opposing viewpoints. Students are thus taught that public critical judgment is unacceptable because even the most uninformed idea, shouted loud enough, deserves equal time with far-better-developed ideas. If we are not careful, American schoolchildren in the twenty-first century will be taught that the evolutionary critique of creationism is a "personal judgment."

Finally, modern philosophy and intellectual discourse have succumbed to the brokering style. Softened up by the Western tradition's disdain for everyday experience, and lacking the independence of life and mind that comes from having a solid grounding in primary experience, many modern professors are little more than intellectual brokers. For decades, so-called analytic philosophy, the very image of intellectual brokering, has dominated university classrooms and textbooks in the United States. This philosophy takes as its goal the analysis of language and argument, nothing more. The idea is to show which arguments or claims might succeed—"go through" (to the end), as intellectuals put it—regardless of the meaning of the positions. The ability to develop claims, counterclaims, and arguments on any and all sides of issues has become the goal of many philosophers. Richard Rorty asserts that "a nation can count itself lucky to have several thousand relatively leisured and relatively unspecialized intellectuals who are exceptionally good at putting together arguments and taking them apart again."[7] Theorists who spend their days focusing on the structure of arguments and ignoring those arguments' human import soon lose sight of the worries of people who are more concerned with meaning than structure. No doubt casuistry is a desirable skill, but it makes a poor goal in life. Think of the goals of some of the classic philosophers: to help people discover what is right, true, or beautiful.

### BEYOND AUTHENTICITY

Because so much of what I have said about modern experience in this book has been of a critical nature, it is important to make it clear that modern experience has some pluses and that even the brokering style has some virtues. For if we are to forge a program for reintroducing experience, we need to know what is available for us to work with.

The best brokers treat all customers equally. (They will say that they treat all people equally, but of course they don't treat poor people the same way they treat rich people.) And brokers will try to turn all people into their customers. The intellectual virtue of the broker, therefore, is not his unwillingness to judge but his generally distributed skepticism: let everyone come to me, and I shall withhold judgment on them all equally. Bertolt Brecht pinpointed this skepticism in one his greatest poems, "In Praise of Doubt":

> Praised be doubt! I advise you to greet
> Cheerfully and with respect the man
> Who tests your word like a bad penny
> I'd like you to be wise and not to give
> Your word with too much assurance.[8]

When used correctly, Cartesian skepticism and the modern "analyze all arguments equally" philosophy can have the value of objectifying our thoughts and helping us see where we might be going wrong. Of course, to use this skepticism wisely one must apply it to oneself as well as to others. The greatest virtue of modernity lies in this self-honesty, or authenticity, as Charles Taylor, surely the most thoughtful defender of modernity, calls it.[9]

In his poem Brecht shows how a modern brokering skepticism that lacks this honesty can destroy itself. First, we become likely to doubt other people's experience, privileging our own as sacrosanct:

> There are the thoughtless who never doubt.
> Their digestion is splendid, their judgment infallible.
> They don't believe in the facts, they believe only in
>     themselves. When it comes to the point
> The facts must go by the board. Their patience with
>     themselves
> Is boundless. To arguments
> They listen with the ear of a police spy.

Lacking self-honesty, such "spies" use the modern critique of experience to undermine others, not to change themselves. For these people, authenticity does not go far enough.

But honesty and authenticity can also go too far. We can worry so much about the degradation of experience that we fall into a state of continual self-doubt. In this condition, we become unable to gain real experience and are cast adrift:

> The thoughtless who never doubt
> Meet the thoughtful who never act.
> They doubt, not in order to come to a decision but
> To avoid a decision. Their heads
> They use only for shaking. With anxious faces
> They warn the crews of sinking ships that water is
> > dangerous.

Written in the late 1930s, Brecht's poem was responding to the cultural crisis brought about by the Nazis. Indeed, European civilization was then a sinking ship, and many of the most articulate intellectuals did little more than murmur something, as Brecht put it, "about the situation not yet being clarified" while countless others, especially in business and the arts, acquired the intellectual habits of police spies.

Brecht's prescience is brought home strikingly in research conducted by Paul Loeb on political involvement (or lack of it) among college students in the United States. Loeb found that the majority of students he studied resembled Brecht's overly thoughtful doubters—they claimed to want to be active politically, but they were waiting, as Loeb puts it, for the Absolutely Perfect cause. Since it doesn't exist, the students never found a cause worthy of acting on, despite their (private) judgment that they would like to be more involved. Most of these students could be characterized as liberal. In contrast, conservative activists interviewed by Loeb often self-consciously forged themselves into true believers (and in not a few cases became spies, reporting on the activities of other students and teachers). Interestingly, in the one case where Loeb interviewed some liberal true believers (militants who closed down several campuses in the student strike against the City University of New York), Loeb blames them for undermining the self-confidence of the liberal "rank and file" because of the militants' vocal public judgments about the importance of the strike.[10] Apparently Loeb himself believes it is bad to be "judgmental" in public.

In times of crisis, like the late 1930s in Germany or among highly motivated young adults, like those in Loeb's research, the brokering style offers only extreme choices: the cynic, the spy, or the fearful neutral. In calmer times, the shortcomings of both the self-righteous and the indecisive are less poignant. Yet even in the calmest of times, the brokering style ultimately leads to a closed experience. Neither true believers nor self-doubters can embrace novel experience and its meaning. Their experience becomes increasingly static and flat; they lack what I call love of life.

Taylor's analysis of this closedness or flatness in experience seems to me correct. He notes that most proponents of modernism have equated the self-honesty of authenticity with the absence of a viewpoint—similar to the myth of the neutral objectivity of the media or in the writing of history. Taylor argues that this attitude is self-defeating; indeed, it is self-eliminating, because one cannot develop and grow through experience into a rich self without embracing viewpoints, defending them against criticisms, and improving or even changing them when necessary. Judgment does not undermine authenticity, poor judgment does, or judgment used for bad purposes. Authenticity requires us to develop a viewpoint (or, more commonly, multiple viewpoints) so that judgment and experience can help us grow into honest selves. Someone who is afraid of being judgmental will tend to avoid opportunities for serious debate and discussion. By keeping her judgments to herself she inhibits the growth of her own experience, denying herself the important experience of genuine give-and-take with others who want to share their differing experiences. Such private, untested judgments tend to be thin and lacking in perspective because diverging perspectives on an issue can be coordinated only through a genuine sharing of experience. This brings us back, once again, to Dewey's emphasis on lived experience and its growth within a social context.

Taylor's attempt to save what is valid in modernized experience thus points us in the same direction as Dewey's critique of brokerism. But although Dewey and Taylor both emphasize the importance of growth in experience, neither has much to say about what that growth might be. Once again, we need to turn to Gibson's ecological psychology.

### THE GROWTH OF EXPERIENCE

One of the most important aspects of human awareness is our ability to extend our experience into the future. As we learn to move we also learn to see that the most distant vistas within our field of view are not static edges at the end of the world but surfaces that conceal new, as-yet-unexplored places. We begin to see not only where we are heading but where we shall go. At first our control of our movements may well be limited to setting paths within the realm of what is visible from here and now. But even a toddler soon learns how to orient toward hidden goals. Here again the human penchant for sharing experience plays an important role. It is often through secondhand experience that we learn to set our goals. A three-year-old has no difficulty when she is told that the toy she wants is in another room—she easily orients to the now-hidden goal, makes the intervening vistas open up in the correct order, and comes upon what she wants. This is no mean feat (it still totally bamboozles the people who make robots), and despite its apparent simplicity, it is paradigmatic of how human experience is prospective and open to growth.

Finding the toy in another room usually requires the integration of first- and secondhand experience, what philosophers call tacit and explicit knowing. Being told that the toy is in another room gives the child explicit knowledge or information; she now knows a fact about the location of the toy. Yet she can make use of this explicit knowledge only with the help of tacit knowledge: her perceptual skills, which help her orient herself to both her immediate and the more distant environment by making the optic flow such that the patterns of progressive occlusion and disocclusion specify a path toward the goal. This is knowledge we rarely think about but without which we could not function.

Because all observation represents an active search for information and takes place in a complex environment, it has this "will-lead-to-ness" about it. As we explore the information available to us—with our eyes, ears, nose, mouth, and hands or various combinations thereof—we are automatically monitoring not only the information immediately available but also what comes next. Psychologists Claes von Hofsten and David Lee call this phenomenon *prospective control*.[11] In their studies of perceptually guided action they have found that prospectivity is fundamental. All experience, even that of newborns or animals like spiders and flies, is prospective. Perhaps Dewey dimly saw what they have now demonstrated: once perceiving is tied to acting, it is less helpful to represent the world as it is than to anticipate imminent changes in one's surroundings. The best mental model of the world is of no use to a moving child who cannot anticipate the rapid changes in her center of gravity and keeps falling down.

In a flowing array of environmental information we find information about what we are doing now, but but we also find information about what *might* happen, about what is imminent. An observer can use the focus of expansion to determine what she will run into unless she changes course. (It can also tell her how much time she has until the crash.) Changing patterns of occlusion tell an observer what objects will come into sight if she continues on her course. Our experience is thus alive with possibility and potentiality, not for an internal observer to make hypothetical judgments but for an active observer to notice imminent developments. Learning is the growth of this kind of experience.

Further, we can become aware of how to control our actions in order to make the imminent actual. The toddler is aware that a ball can be kicked, but she usually falls down when trying to kick it until she learns to control prospectively the changes in balance that she realizes will occur when she starts to kick.

A great deal of both prospective awareness and control is based on firsthand, tacit knowledge. Nobody can tell you all the things you need to be aware of in order to kick a ball; you must discover them for yourself. But secondhand, explicit knowledge can play a useful role as well. Its most important job is to call attention to things ("Try this. See, you can kick it!"). Often our goals (even our paths) are made explicit, although how we reach them is almost always based on implicit knowledge and skill. The fundamental value of primary experience is that it is prospective, containing within it glimmerings of paths to possible futures.

### VALUING EXPERIENCE, VALUING DEMOCRACY

We hold nothing in this world so dear as our own experience and capacities. Yet, on the whole, we do little to promote the growth of this experience, and the reality of our everyday lives often inhibits its growth. Our democratic system is based, at least in part, on the premise that we all benefit from taking into account each person's experience when making decisions. But nowhere is the shallowness of modern philosophy's commitment to democracy better exposed than in the matter of valuing experience. We have become so muddled about the relation between first- and secondhand experience that we no longer know how to think about the role of the individual in a democracy.

Increasingly, democracy has come to mean little more than a system in which we are given fragmented opportunities for registering isolated opinions. This reduces experience from an active, developmental process to, at best, a static cross section of points of view. Related to this are the brokering-style myth that democracy means all opinions are equal and a deep-rooted unease and unwillingness to consider the concept of wisdom, the idea that a person can, through experience, gain something others might lack. The opposition between democracy and wisdom is pernicious and fallacious, but it is reinforced by our brokering style of life.

There is nothing wrong with the registration of opinions as such. Voting and opinion polling are necessary—even desirable—social functions. But if the registering of opinions occurs in a vacuum, in a social situation in which people do not come together to work on projects related to those opinions and to discuss their merits, then the exercise of democracy becomes attenuated and meaningless.[12] All real, thick human meaning comes from the active experience of people working together. Debate and representation (secondhand experience) divorced from social processes (the problems being discussed and their contexts) tend to lose substance, as no observer of the contemporary scene can have failed to notice.

Worse, the opposition lies not between having and not having experience relevant to group activity but between good and bad experience—between experience that promotes growth and that which inhibits it. William Morris noticed this a century ago when he was thinking about "popularity" in art: "The ordinary man in the street . . . is not unsophisticated. On the contrary, he is steeped in the mere dregs of all the Arts that are current at the time he lives. . . . There is a tendency for all people to fall under the domination of traditions of some sort; and the fine tradition, the higher tradition, having disappeared, men will certainly fall into the power of the lower, and inferior tradition."[13]

Morris's comment will inevitably be read as elitist nowadays, especially with its reference to a higher tradition. But such a reading is mistaken. Morris referred, as he made clear time and again, to a tradition in which artistic production is widely distributed to ordinary people. His love of the Gothic stemmed from the fact that the masons and other manual workers designed the buildings; they did not merely carry out the plans of the architects. How many citizens in the 1990s can say that they have had much experience with this kind of "higher tradition"?

Morris's higher tradition will thus please no modern schools of thought. The conservative elitists who bemoan our loss of standards in both art and ethics would agree with the form of his words, but they would be appalled to discover that the standards Morris wished to promote were to come from ordinary people and that as far as Morris was concerned the tradition could easily do without architects, planners, critics, or professional politicians. But Morris's views would also appall the brokers of artistic or moral judgment. For Morris, experience revealed that each art form, and each kind of moral action, had standards that could not be overlooked or gainsaid. The idea that either art or morals should be a vehicle for mere self-expression was to him the highest form of degradation, the detestable outgrowth of a marketplace mentality and a brokering style. Perhaps he saw something that many of us have missed.

I suggest that what he saw—and what virtually everyone in the twentieth century has missed—was that not all work is good. Morris speaks of "useful work versus useless toil" and attacks the "creed of modern morality" that all labor is by definition good. He notes that this is a convenient belief for "those who live on the labor of others." In the late twentieth century many of us live on the labor of others; virtually all of us who have a public voice do so, and we would do well to remember Morris's admonition. For Morris, useful work was, above all, work that inculcated pride and hope: pride in one's self and one's product, hope for self-improvement and sufficient "rest." Labor becomes something one can turn to eagerly, with a desire for self-improvement. Useless work, on the other hand, results in products "not worth making" or which must be made by "labor degrading to the makers."[14] Nothing should be made solely for profit. This robs us of our pride. And work that is so intense or so unpleasant as to prevent either hope or pride is also degrading.

Morris's ideas about work came not merely through historical and philosophical reflection, although he did plenty of that; they derived in large part from primary experience. Morris himself revived many lost crafts and skills, including several kinds of dyeing and glass staining and rug weaving. He created a commercial building and decorating firm in which he trained artisans and through which he promoted his ideals. His attempt to do good work within his society radicalized his social views.[15] From 1871 until his death in 1896, he came into daily conflict between doing things the right way and the demands of the market. In particular, he saw that the financial success of his firm often depended upon cheapening the labor, both by reducing wages and by substituting poor work for good work.

After a career of great accomplishment as a poet, craftsman, and capitalist, Morris's frustration with the existing order erupted. What made life worthwhile for him was hope and pride in his self and his work—the values of everyday experience—and these he could not effectively promote, even for his own employees. He joined and even began to lead the most radical organizations in support of working people, himself working tirelessly, organizing and speechifying all over England, Scotland, and Wales. Morris's message was consistent: much of the drudgery of modern work comes from its disconnection from the real values of ordinary experience. If workers were allowed to make quality products, to use their own abilities and experience to the utmost, then much of the dreariness of their toil could be eliminated.

Morris was not a utopian. He knew that effecting such major changes in everyday life would require worker control of even the biggest enterprises to make products for use, not profit. He knew this was asking for revolutionary change, but he also knew that one of the strongest motives toward such a change is that only when such changes come will technology be a help-meet in work, instead of a constraint. Furthermore, he knew that there were sites within the modern world that afforded the beginnings of such changes. Specialty production, where the artistic talent of a craft shop is part of what sells the product, for example, offers a small window of opportunity within the monolithic market, and it was this window that Morris tried to keep open in his own enterprises.

Morris also rightly saw that with enough organization and will, even modern factories could be made into sites for changing and improving experience. Here he anticipated (and went well beyond) some of the best developments of modern cooperative workplaces. In his speech "A Factory as It Might Be," Morris told the workers of the 1880s that learning is a lifelong process, requiring a healthy environment and an appropriate amount of time for self-development.[16] He suggested that factories could be set amid parks and playgrounds (he does not mention gyms, but the idea is there), with workers getting time off each day for exercise and recreation. He believed that educators would wish to use such factories as places to offer instruction in a variety of skills and arts, both to relieve the tedium of the working day and to expand the horizons of the common people, making them more valuable citizens and workers. When asked by his incredulous and impoverished listeners how these paradisial factories might be paid for, Morris smiled and pointed out that factories were already paying for several such country clubs, but the clubs were situated far away from the workplace, at the homes of the managers and owners. The same is true today, although the worksites are often built in different countries from the pleasant country club estates. If anything, constraint and supervision of workers has increased since Morris's day. We need to recover his vision of human dignity and to fight not only for jobs but for jobs that facilitate growth.

To contrast Morris's ideas and efforts with those of recent artists and philosophers is to grow ashamed of our late twentieth-century smugness. If art, experience, and philosophy are truly valuable, then where are our efforts to make not the products of these but the process and experience of them accessible to as many people as possible? It is far easier for a student to receive what amounts to a free college education by being a good football player than by being a good student, and yet I have never heard of an organized effort by university professors to redress this absurd situation.

Great scholars and researchers like Thomas Henry Huxley (a contemporary of Morris's) made extraordinary efforts to teach working people at adult-education and workers' schools, despite their busy schedules. The few such efforts I know of in our day are largely run by devoted radicals, with little assistance from academia. Nearly every high school and college teacher I have met in the past decade has bemoaned the decline of reading among their students. Yet almost none of these teachers has joined in efforts to limit television watching, which is widely understood to be the first step toward solving the problem. On the whole, academics and other educators have been seduced by an elitist worldview that has prevented them from believing well enough of personal experience and its wisdom to strive to share it as widely as possible.

It is a conceit of philosophers like Rorty to speak of philosophy as a "great conversation," but who do they think they're kidding? Have any UAW members been invited to chat lately? How about migrant farm workers, who are likely to have some interesting observations on the nature of the environment and the meaning of borders? For that matter, what about the local fundamentalist church women's club? If we wait for these folks to enter the academic conversation, we will be waiting until doomsday. Moreover, if we insist that they enter the conversation on our terms, we shall just be perpetuating the anti-experiential bias of our modern Western tradition. If this is a conversation, why is it that we academics are not truly interested in what other folks have to say about their experiences? Morris went on tour to listen as well as to talk, and he always claimed that what he heard strengthened his work. He had a genuine appetite to learn from the experience of others, an appetite we would do well to cultivate.

Christopher Lasch suggests that we modern elites believe in information only as something that *we* can dispense, that will *preclude* argument, not open discussion. The idea is that if "we educate them" they will—inevitably? miraculously?—come to take our side in debates. This debased and passive concept of information now pervades our society, so that even popular political action groups (of all persuasions) seem to have forgotten that experience is the result of debate, argument, and discussion; that the detection and use of information is an *active* process. Modern academia in particular has certainly forgotten this, as one sees in the proliferation of stances and positions taken and in the decrease in serious, open debate. But Lasch gets it right: "The attempt to bring others around to our own point of view carries the risk, of course, that we may adopt their point of view instead. . . . Argument is risky and unpredictable, therefore educational."[17]

We do not have to disagree with Rorty that philosophy is a kind of conversation, but we must make sure that we are not just talking to ourselves. Like Morris, we must learn to learn from experience, even that of the humble and downtrodden. As Morris knew, one wins the right and the ability to teach only after one has shown a genuine openness to learning.

Those who call Morris a dreamer or a utopian—and this is the typical reaction to his ideas—are wrong. Compared to other writers in the arts (even compared to many writers on social issues), Morris had a great deal of firsthand experience with the problems of work. What his experience showed him was the intense conflict between a competitive marketplace and the creation of conditions for good work. Even "well-intentioned" capitalists (like himself) did not have the power to resolve this conflict, nor did labor-saving machines (which Morris tried) help.

The century since Morris wrote has amply confirmed his experience and added to it. As historian Asa Briggs notes, Morris's ideas offer a critique of twentieth-century communism as well as of capitalism.[18] In both systems the problem is one of too little democracy in daily life, the result of an unnecessarily extensive division of labor, especially between mental and physical work. Since Morris's day a number of cultural factors has tended to increase these problems.

Worse, the nihilism that is born of the degrading division of labor has led to attitudes that further the destruction of the environment, and even promote war. If any work at all is considered good work, then even work that causes pollution or the mass-production of weapons will be seen as essential to the economy. How many Americans right now are convinced both that they are lucky to have their jobs and that their work is dangerous to their own or other people's well-being? "It is luckiest," Morris wrote, when our products "have done nobody any good; for oftenest they have done many people harm, and we have toiled and groaned and died in making poison and destruction for our fellow men."[19] The past half-century has seen astronomical increases in the production of pollutants, poisons, and especially weapons. Changes in this production for destruction will be among the most difficult to implement because of the power of these markets in our modern economy.

To the charge of elitism that was often raised against his demand of art for everyone, Morris had a ready answer: Allow people to be educated as they see fit, and make education as widely available as possible, not just to children. Allow people to work in dignity, without coercion through fear (whether of the state or of destitution). Allow workers a say in their materials and procedures. Give people time to assimilate these changes and to learn to work together, to discuss, debate, alter, change, and rethink. Then it will be time to assess what people choose to make and how they make it. After this, let us renew the debate over values and standards. Through this process a new "high tradition" could be created, although Morris did not underestimate the difficulty of creating it: "It is right and necessary that all men should have work to do which shall be worth doing, and be of itself pleasant to do; and which should be done under such conditions as would make it neither overwearisome nor overanxious. Turn that claim about as I may . . . I cannot find it . . . exorbitant. . . . Yet . . . if society would or could admit it, the face of the world would be changed."[20] Above all, what would be changed in Morris's new world would be the spread of hope, the precondition of which is meaningful work that allows us to develop our own experience.

### HOPE

Because all human experience, from the simplest stroll to the most complex technical skill, carries limitless possibilities, the most important aspect of our experience, hope, is not a subjective feeling but an objective property of our encounters with the world. In its broadest sense, hope means that a goal is *achievable*. In present terms, hope is part of our experience when we detect information that tells us how to reach a goal. It is not enough for the information to be available, it must be detected. Often a goal can be perceived without understanding how it will be achieved; this leads, at best, to fantasy, not hope. The child who sees a desirable toy on television can fantasize about getting it, but only the older child—who knows how to find the shop (and perhaps how to talk his parent into paying)—can actually hope to get the toy.

Hope can be inarticulate. It is rooted in direct, not secondhand, experience. We often perceive both goals and the means of achieving them without having explicit knowledge of the process. Many self-taught skills fit into this pattern, where one just "does it" without being able to explain how the goal can be achieved or even, in some cases, without being aware that a goal was achieved. Many children who have had a difficult upbringing learn self-reliance and all manner of skills but still think of themselves as needy and dependent. (This can be true even when the children are less needy and dependent than their parents.) It may need a persistent friend or counselor to awaken such children to their own experience of autonomy and skill. The psychologist Martin Seligman has shown that repeated, explicit labeling of things that are the result of one's own actions as due to others or to external forces can induce a general attitude of anti-hope, of what he calls learned helplessness.[21] People who label things in this way do not need to change their actions as much as they need to get in touch with their firsthand experience of competence and capability and to resist the secondhand misdesignation of their abilities.

We have undermined the hopeful components of experience by eliminating its objective nature. Because of the machining of the mind, the potentiality inherent in personal experience is interpreted subjectively, rather than as something that offers the possibility for change. Increasingly in modern society, people seek to change themselves, and they decreasingly imagine significant changes in their external circumstances. The modern perspective allows self-esteem or self-aggrandizement but not true hope.[22] One can work at achieving a strong self-image, but that image is always an idea or an ideal, a subjective model of reality. Most of us have little experience in planning and implementing genuine changes in our circumstances on a daily basis. Self-image as such does not include the kind of agency needed to change things and thereby create hope. Except in the mythology of "self-help" literature, self-images cannot guide us through life because life choices demand real abilities and skills. When a self-image expands in the absence of hope, this is by no means a healthy thing. Juvenile delinquents who have little genuine cause for hope (many expect to die violent deaths in the near future) often score high on tests of self-esteem. They recognize in themselves real power and ability but have no perception of a constructive path for self-growth.[23]

Here again, Dewey seems to have been prescient. Hope is neither subjective nor private. It is an aspect of public experience and public action. Hope requires that individuals perceive both their successes and their capabilities as agents and also that the paths to their goals are "open" (within reach of their kind of agency).[24] To inculcate this kind of experience would require the kind of democratization of experience that both Morris and Dewey promoted, including a far more radical democratization of school and work than has ever been attempted. Access to resources of all kinds—educational, vocational, and professional—would have to be broadened. The concept of education itself should be broadened, to encompass facilitating the growth of experience in all aspects of life, not just schooling as such.

A good example of how schooling can extend beyond the classroom and help democratize the experience of an entire community is the Central Park East Schools project spearheaded by Deborah Meier and her colleagues.[25] Working in public schools (first at the elementary level, and then extending from kindergarten through twelfth grade) Meier demonstrates that education begins with the community and with noncognitive processes. Her group's procedure has been to carve out small "schools" (often purely functional entities, housed within larger school buildings—the legacy of our society's penchant for warehouse school buildings). These smaller entities can be run with an emphasis on, first, respect for the individual child and his or her experiences and, second, democratic process: allowing the voices of the children and their families to be a central part of making the schools work. Meier is adamant that in modern American society, with its diversity and strong centrifugal forces pulling at children, one cannot even begin to educate a community unless schooling is based on respect for the dignity of persons. I would add that this emphasis in turn does what is most educationally needful for the children: it teaches them to value their own experience and to make something of themselves on the basis of that experience. The educational achievements of students in these schools is notably better than that of their peers elsewhere in the New York City school system. And, even more important, the schools have become not just a beacon but an actual pathway to hope for many in the community.

The seeds of hope are thus to be found within the homely aspects of modern daily life. Charles Taylor is right: the modern approach to experience provides us with a basis for hope. Yet Taylor fails to specify the most important component available to us for producing hope—learning to respect the experience of others. (Although I suspect that this is what he has in mind when he emphasizes the importance of "authenticity" in our dealings with others.) Without succumbing to a bland, brokering style, we must nevertheless learn how to value openness to others and how to encourage mutual respect and a genuine sharing of experience. If we are forced to choose between the uncertainties of Taylor's openness and Rorty's more cozy, closed discourses, we should choose the former.

The ecological concept of experience I am promoting can add a great deal to this ethic of authenticity. Taylor understands that openness should not prevent us from either developing a perspective from which to judge others or striving to encourage growth, even among those with whom we are in conflict. But Taylor cannot *explain* why this should be so. I have argued that the growth of personal experience is necessarily social, as well as individual, and that therefore a combination of accrued wisdom and genuine openness is a realistic goal.

Second, modern philosophers and scientists need to junk their obsessive fear of uncertainty—a fear that has erected a barrier between academic concerns and everyday life. The example of the pragmatists and the emerging ecological approach to psychology gives us a platform for doing this without abandoning rigorous standards of evidence or analysis. It is striking that outside of academia thinkers like Morris or Lewis Mumford have been able to make influential connections between the problems of daily life and theories of art, morals, and knowledge. I hope that my radical rethinking of the concept of experience may stimulate at least some movement among academics back toward the homely problems of daily life.

Finally, we need to look not toward *a* vision of the future but toward *many* visions, each rooted in firsthand experience as well as in theory and talk. Intellectuals can bring their skills of analysis and communication—of secondhand experience—to the task of articulating the many possibilities found in primary experience, but they must first bring the two kinds of experience together in ways that have yet to be invented. We need especially to learn Taylor's lesson of balancing our own adherence to a particular viewpoint with an openness to alternatives. We live in a crowded world, and there are many paths into the future. Can we work together to find the more hopeful paths?

# EPILOGUE    Fighting for Experience

This book is about how we are losing our minds. I don't mean that we are all going insane but that, collectively, we are allowing our mental resources to erode. The ability to experience the world around us accurately and to use this experience to think carefully is, I claim, a casualty of current trends in work, education, and everyday life. Worse, the way philosophers and psychologists have taught us to think about our mental life seriously underestimates the value of experience. In their refusal to value experience as they ought, intellectuals and educators have added to rather than ameliorated the problem.

The kind of experience I defend here against the onslaught of various social forces is nothing fancy. Primary experience consists simply of what we can see, feel, taste, hear, or smell for ourselves. But it is the basis of all our mental life. And being alive to what occurs around us is the basis of existence. We are all born with the ability to explore our environment and carry within ourselves tremendous possibilities for learning and growth through experience. Yet our society seems bent on squandering these opportunities.

Any skill, from driving a car to playing an instrument to painting or acting, requires the ability to master one's experience. Indeed, merely enjoying something (food, sex, or a sunset) requires that ability. To interact well with others, whether in casual encounters or complex social affairs, we must use the astuteness we have gained from experience to understand, anticipate, and respond appropriately to the feelings and actions of others. Clear, careful thinking begins with the ability to evaluate experience, to make distinctions, identify causes, and watch for patterns and trends. Moreover, doing any of these things well requires considerable time, effort, and opportunity. In sum, it is not too much to say almost everything that makes life worth living begins in experience and grows with it.

Throughout this book I have emphasized that everyday experience is something that each of us has and can get more of. But this does not make all experience equal. Experience can be shaped, refined, and improved. Through practice and effort some people become more capable of apprehending and understanding certain things than are others. Everyone deserves a certain amount of respect, and we should acknowledge the basic respect due to all people—but further respect must be earned. When people exercise their power to *make something* of their experience, it calls forth acknowledgment from others.

Honoring people for their special skills, understanding, and competence—for having made something of their experience—is not elitist. Elitists tend to define such special abilities as a way of erecting barriers. But diversity of experience is the soul of community life and should never be used as an excuse for creating barriers. Indeed, if special experiences are not shared, then what value do they have? The disdain of twentieth-century intellectuals for everyday experience has made it difficult for them to share their concerns widely. Many of the artists who rejected Morris's call for a return to the everyday sneered at the idea that their work could be "appreciated" by the crowd. As Christopher Lasch shows, this elitism has also been endemic among twentieth-century intellectuals, scientists, and artists. It is gratifying, then, to find the following defense of art as a means of integrating experience and everyday life from perhaps the greatest twentieth-century painter, Pablo Picasso:

> What do you think an artist is? A half-wit with nothing but eyes if he is a painter, ears if he is a musician, lyres installed on every floor if he is a poet, or just muscles and nothing else if he happens to be a boxer? Far, far from it: at the same time he is also a political being, keenly and perpetually aware of the heartbreaking or passionate or delightful things that happen in the world, and he molds himself entirely in their likeness. How could you conceivably cut yourself off from other men and from the life they bring you in such abundance? In the name of what uncaring, ivory-tower kind of attitude? No: painting is not there merely to decorate the walls of flats. It is a means of waging offensive and defensive war against the enemy.[1]

Picasso understood that real art emerges from ordinary experience and cannot be divorced from it. Although his artistic styles and practices could hardly differ more from Morris's, both artists were united in their conviction that art is a necessary way of enriching everyday experience. Both loved to transform their living places, to design rugs and chairs, plates and wall decorations that expressed how they wished to live. As our minds become increasingly machined, as we find ourselves living more and more in the thin air of secondhand experience, we lose this important ability to transform our own experience into something more beautiful, useful, and important. In spite of the much-touted benefits and conveniences of modern life, we see no increase in ordinary people's interest in or capacity to make songs or tapestries, to extend and share their own experiences. Instead, we have let ourselves be inundated with prefabricated (and often ersatz) experience, and this in turn has tended to limit both the ordinary person's experience and his ability to expand and transform that experience on his own terms.

This emphasis on expanding the domain of experience, both within the individual and among individuals, is John Dewey's greatest legacy. When asked why we should prefer democracy to other political systems, Dewey had a ready answer, which amplifies the points made by both Morris and Picasso:

> Can we find any reason [for preferring democracy] that does not ultimately come down to the belief that democratic social arrangements promote a better quality of human experience, one which is more widely accessible and enjoyed, than do non-democratic . . . forms of social life? Does not the principle of regard for individual freedom and for decency and kindliness of human relations come back in the end to the conviction that these things are tributary to a higher quality of experience on the part of a greater number than are methods of repression and coercion or force? Is it not the reason for our preference that we believe that mutual consultation and convictions reached through persuasion, make possible a better quality of experience than can otherwise be provided on any wide scale?[2]

Have we the courage and the stamina to pick up where Morris and Dewey left off? Can we succeed where the pragmatists failed and bring a new view of experience—one rooted in the abundance of life—to our theories and perhaps even to our actions? In the modern climate of cynicism and nihilism it is easy to assert that we can't change people's inclinations and habits. But this is both intellectually and morally lazy. The burden of such historical works as William Leach's on the brokering style is that these new modes of experiencing are cultural constructions, created and disseminated by the tireless efforts of individuals who were trying to change their society. Our greatest artists and philosophers have vouchsafed us a glimpse of a new way of organizing our experience, even of some of the paths we might take to that much-desired goal.

The greatest myth of the twentieth century is that people are sheep. Our elitist intellectual culture has been built on the idea that ordinary people tend to see things as others want them to, with little independence of mind. This is a pernicious assumption. "Let us recognize," James Gibson wrote, "the strength of the dead hand of habit on perception. Let us acknowledge that people—other people, of course—often perceive the world like silly sheep. But it is wrong to make a philosophy of this rather snobbish observation. The orthodox theories of perception have encouraged this fallacy."[3] It was Gibson's purpose to undermine such thinking.

Throughout the past hundred years or more scientists, philosophers, educators, politicians, even artists and writers have falsely assumed that most people cannot see things for themselves and therefore need to be rescued from a sheeplike stupor. Modernist culture has from its outset been enamored of the reliability and power of mechanism; many modernists allied themselves with the trend toward increased automation, believing that the machining of our minds would lead to improvements in our mental performance. The dismal results speak for themselves. Worse, the emerging postmodernist culture—at least as represented by its elite intellectual voices—seems to be responding to modernism's machining of the mind by abandoning the very idea of using our minds to understand our place in the world. Surely it is time to listen to Gibson and relearn the homely lesson that all understanding, no matter how fancy and refined, is rooted in ordinary experience. The meanings of our lives will be found only when we make the effort to look for ourselves.

# NOTES

CHAPTER ONE   Have You Ever Been Experienced?

1  William James, *Essays in Radical Empiricism* (Cambridge: Harvard University Press, 1976). R. B. Perry, E. B. Holt, et al., *The New Realism* (New York: Scribner's, 1912); Herbert Schneider, *American Realism* (Indianapolis: Bobbs-Merrill, 1964). Almost no scholarly attention has been paid to the greatest of the New Realists, James's student E. B. Holt. Holt formalized radical empiricism and integrated it with the emerging discipline of symbolic logic in his *Concept of Consciousness* (New York: Macmillan, 1914), and he related his New Realism to both Freudian theory and modern physiological ideas in his masterpiece, the unjustly neglected *Freudian Wish and Its Place in Ethics* (New York: Holt, 1915). In part because of personal problems with a senior colleague and in part because of tension over his homosexuality, Holt felt compelled to resign from Harvard in 1916; he returned only sporadically to academia. His last important essay, "Materialism and the Criterion of the Psychic," *Psychological Review* 44 (1937): 33–53, offers an important naturalistic account of experience. The only good source on Holt is the fine chapter in Bruce Kuklick, *The Rise of American Philosophy* (New Haven: Yale University Press, 1977). John Dewey's metaphysical ideas are best extracted from his *Experience and Nature* (South Bend, Ind.: Open Court, 1925) and *Art and Experience* (New York: Scribner's, 1931).

2  Arthur Lovejoy, *The Revolt Against Dualism* (South Bend, Ind.: Open Court, 1930); Bertrand Russell, "William James's Conception of Truth," in Russell, *Philosophical Essays* (London: Allen and Unwin, 1910).

3 Terence Irwin, *Classical Thought* (New York: Oxford University Press, 1989), is an excellent overview of classical Greek philosophy.

4 See Nancy Maull, "Cartesian Optics and the Geometrization of Nature," *Review of Metaphysics* 32 (1978): 253–273, and E. S. Reed, "The Corporeal Ideas Hypothesis," *Review of Metaphysics* 34 (1982): 731–752.

5 See Isaac Newton, *The Opticks* (Berkeley: University of California Press, 1932); René Descartes, *The Discourse on Method,* in John Cottingham et al., eds., *The Philosophical Works of Descartes,* vol. 1 (New York: Cambridge University Press, 1985).

6 The most important of Reid's texts related to these issues is not his *Inquiry* of 1764, but his remarkable companion volumes: *The Essays on the Intellectual Powers of Man* (1785) and *The Essays on the Active Powers of Man* (1788). Read together these contain the seeds of both scientistic Enlightenment thinking and much of the post-Enlightenment worldview as well. Both texts are reprinted in William Hamilton, ed., *The Works of Thomas Reid,* 2 vols. (Edinburgh: Maclachlan and Straban, 1872).

7 Easily the best overview of Kant's early influence—and one that clearly outlines the variety of ways his ideas were interpreted—is Frederick Beiser's *Fate of Reason* (Cambridge: Harvard University Press, 1987).

8 Of course, Kant interpretation is exceedingly difficult, and there are reasonable objections to my interpretation here. My goal is not to offer a foolproof interpretation of Kant (could there be such a thing?) but to make the point that few philosophers try to interpret Kant literally or straightforwardly on these matters. Might it not prove useful to do so? Instead, much of Kant scholarship seems bent on making him say things that are congruent with the standard Western anti-experiential line of thought. For example, Patricia Kitcher's *Kant's Psychology* (New York: Oxford University Press, 1993), by the simple expedient of never citing the passage in Kant's first *Critique* concerning empirical realism, makes Kant sound like a modern cognitive scientist who embraces empirical idealism.

9 Arthur Schopenhauer, *The World as Will and Representation,* 2 vols. (New York: Dover, 1978). See especially the appendix to vol. 1, where Schopenhauer offers his appreciative critique of Kant.

10 G. W. F. Hegel, *The Science of Logic,* 2 vols. (London: Allen and Unwin, 1929).

11 For the "unconscious mania" of the 1860s, see E. S. Reed, "Theory, Concept and Experiment in the History of Psychology," *History of the Human Sciences* 4 (1989): 333–353, and *From Soul to Mind: The Emergence of Psychological Ideas, 1815–1890* (New Haven: Yale University Press, forthcoming). For physiological psychology applied to human labor, see Anson Rabinbach, *The Human Motor* (New York: Basic, 1992). For the influence of science on

impressionist painting, see P. Vitz and A. Glimcher, *Modern Art and Modern Science: The Parallel Analysis of Vision* (New York: Praeger, 1984).

12 Giorgio Agamben develops this idea of Walter Benjamin's in *Infancy and History: Essays on the Destruction of Experience,* trans. L. Heron (London: Verso, 1993).

13 William James, *The Principles of Psychology,* 2 vols. (New York: Holt, 1890); James, *Pragmatism: A New Name for Some Old Ways of Thinking,* reprinted in James, *Writings, 1902–1910* (New York: Library of America, 1987). John Dewey, *Reconstruction in Philosophy,* reprinted in *The Middle Works of John Dewey, 1899–1924,* vol. 12 (Carbondale: Southern Illinois University Press, 1988).

14 Richard Rorty, *Philosophy and the Mirror of Nature* (Princeton: Princeton University Press, 1979).

15 Hilary Putnam, "The Dewey Lectures, 1994: Sense, Nonsense, and The Senses: An Inquiry into the Powers of the Human Mind," *Journal of Philosophy* 91, no. 9 (1994): 445–511, p. 454.

16 John McDowell, *Mind and World* (Cambridge: Harvard University Press, 1994). The quotations are from Putnam, "Dewey Lectures," 453 and 457.

17 Putnam, "Dewey Lectures," 454.

18 Ibid., 461 and 464.

19 Bertrand Russell, *The Analysis of Matter* (London: Allen and Unwin, 1927); Putnam, "Dewey Lectures," 468.

20 J. L. A. Austin, *Sense and Sensibilia* (New York: Oxford, 1962).

21 Keith Oatley, in *Perception and Representations* (Brighton, Eng.: Harvester, 1978), explicitly equates perception with hallucination, as did Hyppolite Taine a century ago in his *On Intelligence* (New York: Holt and Williams, 1871). Gibson is the first successfully to draw a clear distinction between perception and hallucination, as will be discussed in Chapter 5. See also James J. Gibson, "On the Relation Between Hallucination and Perception," *Leonardo* 3 (1970): 425–427.

22 See Larry Weiskrantz, *Blindsight* (New York: Oxford University Press, 1987), for a review of the pathological phenomena. The trick to seeing diplopic images (and similar phenomena) is to *not* look at them. (This is why I insist that they are part of special, peculiar ways of looking, not ordinary looking.) When you look at a thing you inevitably focus both eyes on it. But only objects in front of or behind the point on which you focus produce double images. One way to see these images is to focus both eyes on an object hanging on a wall at some distance away. Then slowly move a pencil a few inches in front of your nose without changing your gaze. You should see two translucent images of the pencil. For more discussion of the philosophical implications of diplopic images, see E. S. Reed, "Knowers Talking About the Known," *Synthese* 92 (1992): 9–25.

23 For a brief review of these attempts to find the complete set of sensory atoms, see James J. Gibson, "Lessons from a Century of Sensory Psychology," in Sigmund Koch and David Leary, eds., *A Century of Scientific Psychology* (New York: McGraw-Hill, 1985). For more on adaptation and its implications, see Gibson's "Adaptation with Negative After-Effect," *Psychological Review* 44 (1937): 222–244. On the inventory theory of sensory states, see E. G. Boring, *The Physical Dimensions of Consciousness* (New York: Century, 1933). Boring was a student of Titchener's who did his damndest to save Titchener's sense data theory. In this book he explains why he failed.

24 Putnam, "Dewey Lectures," 464.

25 After this book was written, Charles Taylor—whose earlier work is discussed in Chapter 7—offered what I interpret to be a version of the present argument. Throughout his *Philosophical Arguments* (Cambridge: Harvard University Press, 1995), he suggests that a new view of perception is needed to put philosophers back in touch with everyday concerns. He emphasizes that ordinary perceptual experience is structured in terms of significance: we see what things are good for, what we can do with things (or what they can do to us). In Gibson's jargon, we see "the affordances" of our surroundings.

CHAPTER TWO    The Search for a Philosophy of Experience

1 Richard Rorty, *Contingency, Irony, and Solidarity* (New York: Cambridge University Press, 1989), esp. 73–95.

2 Anna Sewell, *Black Beauty* (New York: Scholastic, 1958), 59.

3 For the precipitous drop over the past century in standards of how people treat one another, see the provocative Amnesty International lecture by Eric Hobsbawm, "Barbarism: A User's Guide," *New Left Review* 206 (1994): 44–54. See also his *The Age of Extremes* (New York: Pantheon, 1995).

4 Rorty, *Contingency,* 189; Rorty's claims about the nature of knowledge are summarized in the introductory essay, "Pragmatism and Post-Nietszchean Philosophy," of his *Essays on Heidegger and Others,* vol. 2 of his *Collected Philosophical Essays* (New York: Cambridge University Press, 1991).

5 Oddly, Rorty argues that Dewey promoted a kind of relativism close to Rorty's own. This is discussed at length in Rorty's *Philosophy and the Mirror of Nature* (Princeton: Princeton University Press, 1979) and his more recent "Dewey Between Hegel and Darwin," in Dorothy Ross, ed., *Modernist Impulses in The Human Sciences 1870–1930* (Baltimore: Johns Hopkins University Press, 1994). But this is a tendentious misreading of Dewey, as was shown by Robert Westbrook in the epilogue to his *John Dewey and American Democracy* (Ithaca: Cornell University Press, 1991). I am much indebted to Westbrook's lucid and cogent overview of Dewey's thought; much of what I say about Dewey's work is based on Westbrook's interpretation.

6 John Dewey, *Reconstruction in Philosophy,* reprinted in *The Middle Works of John Dewey 1899–1924,* vol. 12 (Carbondale: Southern Illinois University Press 1988); Dewey, *The Quest for Certainty* (New York: Putnam's, 1932).

7 The classic discussion of negative freedom can be found in Isaiah Berlin, *Four Essays on Liberty* (New York: Oxford University Press, 1969).

8 John Dewey, *Human Nature and Conduct,* reprinted in *The Middle Works of John Dewey,* vol. 14 (Carbondale: Southern Illinois University Press, 1988), 7. This was first published in 1922. For the concept of flowering, see Dewey, *Art and Experience* (New York: Putnam's, 1931) chap. 1.

9 Hilary Putnam, *Renewing Philosophy* (Cambridge: Harvard University Press, 1992), 2.

10 Dewey, *Human Nature,* 9.

11 See Richard Rorty, *Objectivism, Relativism, and Truth,* vol. 1 of *Collected Philosophical Essays* (New York: Cambridge University Press, 1991).

12 John Dewey, *Logic: The Theory of Inquiry* (New York: Holt, 1938); Dewey, *Essays in Experimental Logic* (New York: Holt, 1916).

13 Rorty, *Objectivism,* 10.

14 Dewey first stated his theory of action in "The Reflex Arc Concept in Psychology," *Psychological Review* 3 (1896): 357–370. Recent developments in physiology and psychology have strengthened, not weakened, Dewey's century-old insight. See E. S. Reed, "An Outline of a Theory of Action Systems," *Journal of Motor Behavior* 14 (1982): 98–134. See also E. S. Reed, *Encountering the World: Towards an Ecological Psychology* (New York: Oxford University Press, 1996), esp. chaps. 5–7. The quotations in this paragraph are from pp. 48 and 47, respectively, of Dewey, *Human Nature.*

15 Dewey, *Essays in Experimental Logic,* 78.

16 This is the theme of Westbrook's marvelous biography, *Dewey and American Democracy.*

17 Dewey, *Human Nature,* 115.

18 Ibid., 41–42.

19 Ibid., 48. See also Dewey, *Democracy and Education* (New York: Free Press, 1944); Dewey, *Experience and Education* (1938), reprinted in *The Later Works of John Dewey,* vol. 13 (Carbondale: Southern Illinois University Press, 1991).

20 Dewey, *Quest for Certainty,* 310–311.

21 Clifford Geertz, "Anti-Anti-Relativism," *American Anthropologist* 86 (1984): 263–278; E. S. Reed, "Knowers Talking About the Known," *Synthese* 92 (1992): 9–25.

22 Quoted from Dewey, *Experience and Nature,* in Putnam, *Renewing Philosophy,* 188.

23 Dewey, *Human Nature,* 19.

CHAPTER THREE    Fear of Uncertainty and the Flight from Experience

1 René Descartes, "Meditations on First Philosophy: Second Meditation," in John Cottingham et al., eds., *The Philosophical Works of René Descartes* (Cambridge: Cambridge University Press, 1986), 21.

2 E. A. Burtt, *The Metaphysical Foundations of Modern Physical Science* (Garden City, N.Y.: Doubleday, 1932), and A. N. Whitehead, *Science and the Modern World* (New York: Free Press, 1925), are the classic accounts of how the scientific revolutionaries attacked ordinary experience as a mere subjective addition to the scheme of things.

3 The best recent review of Descartes's dualism is John Cottingham, *Descartes* (London: Routledge, 1990); the best overview of how dualism literally took the life out of our understanding of nature is Marjorie Grene, *The Knower and the Known* (Berkeley: University of California Press, 1974).

4 I discuss the pragmatists at length in this book, but I have had little to say about the phenomenologists and existential phenomenologists. In certain respects, writers like Heidegger and, especially, Maurice Merleau-Ponty have offered theories that are similar to mine. There is a good introductory discussion of these issues in Grene, *Knower and Known*. See also Stuart Hampshire's *Thought and Action* (London: Chatto and Windus, 1959).

5 David Noble, "Social Choice in Machine Design," in Andrew Zimbalist, ed., *Case Studies in the Labor Process* (New York: Monthly Review Press, 1979), 44.

6 Lewis Mumford, *The Myth of the Machine* (New York: Harcourt, Brace, and World, 1967).

7 More than a century ago, John Stuart Mill noticed that "labor saving devices" never did.

8 Managers and industrialists might be afraid of uncertainty because of the many uncertainties created by the "free market" for which they work. Unwilling to control the market-based chaos around them, they focus obsessively on creating order *within* their domains (within the business enterprise, whose internal structure is never run on free-market principles). Harry Braverman, *Labor and Monopoly Capital: The Degradation of Work in the Twentieth Century* (New York: Monthly Review Press, 1974), offers many insights into the radically different treatment accorded problems of order within the business enterprise from that given to problems of order in markets. Unfortunately, this is too big a topic to be discussed fully here.

9 R. B. Gordon, "Who Turned the Mechanical Ideal into the Mechanical Reality?" *Technology and Culture* 29 (1988): 744–778.

10 Lewis Mumford and many other of the early "regionalists" fully expected that the new electronic power and communications technology of the early twentieth century would create conditions for a less centralized, more flexible

and communitarian work life and culture. They rightly emphasized that this new technology had liberating potential, but they failed to understand that the people and institutions behind the rise of that technology could not "afford" to allow that potential to be developed, as they would then lose control over the technological infrastructure, the workforce, and, of course, the profits. It was on the basis of his terrible disappointment in the transformative power of technology in its own right that Mumford developed his concept of technics (the cultural embodiment and use of technology) as opposed to technology. See his classic work, *Technics and Civilization* (New York: Harcourt, 1938).

11 See T. K. Landauer, *The Trouble with Computers: Usefulness, Usability, and Productivity* (Cambridge, Mass.: MIT Press, 1995).

12 James Howard Kunstler, *The Geography of Nowhere: The Rise and Decline of America's Man-Made Landscape* (New York: Simon and Schuster, 1993), 114.

13 Ibid., 113.

CHAPTER FOUR   The Degradation of Experience in the Modern Workplace

1 See Studs Terkel, *Working* (New York: Signet, 1974).

2 Samuel Beckett, *Company* (London: J. Calder, 1980); see also *How It Is* (New York: Grove, 1964). Beckett wrote his master's thesis on Descartes. Hugh Kenner, in his *The Mechanic Muse* (New York: Oxford University Press, 1987), shows the intimate relation between industrialization and modernist writing. His essay "Beckett Thinking" in that book shows that Beckett was greatly influenced by the fundamental idea of artificial intelligence, that language and thought might somehow be reduced to logical mechanisms, to algorithms.

3 Daniel Dennett, "Recent Work in the Philosophy of Mind," *American Philosophical Quarterly* 15 (1978): 249–263.

4 Franz Kafka, *The Castle* (New York: Knopf, 1954), and *The Trial* (New York: Knopf, 1964); see also Ernst Pawel's *The Nightmare of Reason: A Life of Franz Kafka* (New York: Farrar, Straus, and Giroux, 1984).

5 Henry David Thoreau, "On Civil Disobedience," in *Walden and Other Writings* (New York: Modern Library, 1965), 637–638.

6 John Searle, *Minds, Brains, and Science* (Cambridge: Harvard University Press, 1984).

7 Georg Lukács, *History and Class Consciousness* (1921; Cambridge, Mass.: MIT Press, 1971), 8.

8 Ibid., 89.

9 Karl Marx, *Capital* (Harmondsworth, Eng.: Penguin, 1977), 1:548.

10 Wendell Berry, *The Unsettling of America* (Washington, D.C.: Sierra Club, 1977). See also Berry's *What Are People For?* (San Francisco: North Point Press, 1990).

11 Allan Bloom's *Closing of the American Mind* (New York: Simon and Schus-

ter 1987) was the first in a cluster of books that complained about the lack of shared culture among Americans, especially those born after the baby boom. See also E. D. Hirsch, *Cultural Literacy* (Boston: Houghton Mifflin, 1987).

12  William Morris, in May Morris, *Selected Speeches of William Morris* (London: Routledge, 1936), 343.

13  See David F. Norton, *Democracy and Moral Development* (Princeton: Princeton University Press, 1991), for a progressive critique.

14  James Beniger, *The Control Revolution: The Technological and Economic Origins of the Information Society* (Cambridge: Harvard University Press, 1986), 125.

15  As was discussed in the previous chapter, the idea that information technology (or any technology, for that matter) is introduced solely because it increases productivity is a myth. At present, there is no evidence that increases in productivity have materialized from informatization. Indeed, the overwhelming evidence is that industrial managers do not even care to study or document putative increases. David Noble, a historian of technology, tried without success to find a single empirical study proving that the adoption of computerization in the 1970s and 1980s had increased manufacturing productivity (see his *Progress Without People* [Chicago: Charles Kerr, 1994]). Similarly, empirical studies of service industries have primarily been performed by outsiders to the industry and have not shown significant productivity increases. For data on computers and their lack of contribution to increased productivity, see T. K. Landauer, *The Trouble with Computers: Usefulness, Usability, and Productivity* (Cambridge, Mass.: MIT Press, 1995), and R. D. Hays, "Digital displays: RSI and Restructuring Capital." In J. Brook and I. Boal, eds., *Resisting the Virtual Life* (San Francisco: City Lights, 1995).

16  Quoted in Shoshana Zuboff, *In the Age of the Smart Machine* (New York: Basic, 1988), 135.

17  Ibid.

18  Barbara Rogoff, *Apprenticeship in Thinking* (New York: Oxford University Press, 1990), 56.

19  Richard Rorty, *Philosophy and the Mirror of Nature* (Princeton: Princeton University Press, 1979), 61.

20  See Agamben, *Infancy and History: Essays on the Destruction of Experience,* trans. L. Heron (London: Verso, 1993).

21  John Dewey, *The Quest for Certainty* (New York: Putnam's, 1929).

22  Michael Argyle, *The Psychology of Work* (Harmondsworth, Eng.: Penguin, 1989), 31.

23  Adam Smith, *The Wealth of Nations* (New York: Oxford University Press), 781–782.

24  See Doug Henwood, "Information Fetishism," in Brook and Boal, *Resisting the Virtual Life.* Henwood reviews data on the thirty fastest-growing oc-

cupations in the United States: of the top half dozen, only nursing could be considered an education-intensive career. The other rapidly increasing professions, which already account for at least three and a half million workers, are retail-sales jobs, cash-register operation, office work, truck driving, and food-service work.

25  H. H. Rosenbrock, *Machines with a Purpose* (New York: Oxford University Press), 149.

26  This story is told in David Noble, *Progress Without People*. For a detailed history of how all the options for using computer-based machine-shop technology for worker control were undermined by managers and corporation-hired, university-based "experts," see Noble's *Forces of Production* (New York: Knopf, 1987).

27  Rosenbrock, *Machines with a Purpose,* 149. After making this point, Rosenbrock presents a case study of a numerically controlled machine shop in Nebraska that hired mentally handicapped workers.

28  Daniel Dennett, *Elbow Room: The Varieties of Free Will Worth Having* (Cambridge, Mass.: MIT Press, 1984).

29  See Harry Braverman, *Labor and Monopoly Capital: The Degradation of Work in the Twentieth Century* (New York: Monthly Review Press, 1974).

30  Barbara Garson, *The Electronic Sweatshop* (New York: Viking Penguin, 1988), chap. 3. All quotations in this discussion are from this chapter.

31  Many of those who write on the new information technology seem to be enamored of the process of separating experience from decision making. Invariably, they refer to it as a freeing up of workers to think about matters other than the work in front of them. Dissociating thought from work could be seen as liberating only by people who were uninvolved in the work process. For a strong statement of this point of view, backed by extensive sociopsychological analysis, see Zuboff, *In the Age of the Smart Machine.*

32  The first commercial use of most newly introduced information technologies has been an increase in the monitoring and supervision of workers, typically under the rubric of "inventory control" (or "flow management" in service industries). See Landauer, *Trouble with Computers.*

CHAPTER FIVE    Sharing Experience

1  Charles Darwin was the first to show experimentally how perceptive worms are about the soil in which they live and move: see E. S. Reed, "Darwin's Worms: A Case Study in Evolutionary Psychology," *Behaviorism* 10 (1982): 162–185. For an overview of the emerging field of ecological psychology, which deals with these functional relations between animals and the environment, see Reed, *Encountering the World: Towards an Ecological Psychology* (New York: Oxford University Press, 1996).

2 This does not mean that a observer can always obtain the information she wants. No matter how much scrutiny an untrained observer gives to my guitar, she will not be able to discover that the soundbox is made of spruce without some prior experience with various forms of wood. Nevertheless, even an untrained observer can discover an endless number of important things about a guitar, as the playing of many brilliant self-taught musicians shows.

3 James J. Gibson, *The Ecological Approach to Visual Perception* (Boston: Houghton Mifflin, 1979). See also E. S. Reed, *James J. Gibson and the Psychology of Perception* (New Haven: Yale University Press, 1988).

4 Gibson, *Ecological Approach,* 233.

5 D. N. Lee et al., "Common Principles of Guidance by Echolocation and Vision," *Journal of Comparative Physiology* A, 171 (1992): 563–571. See also Reed, *Encountering the World,* chap. 4.

6 J. J. Gibson, G. Kaplan, H. Reynolds, and K. Wheeler, "The Change from Visible to Invisible: A Study in Optical Transitions" (1969), reprinted in E. Reed and R. Jones, eds., *Reasons for Realism: Selected Essays of James J. Gibson* (Hillsdale, N.J.: Erlbaum, 1982).

7 To some degree, the goal (not yet reached) of virtual-reality devices is to provide realistic patterns of occlusion that track the exploratory movements of the observer. This does not invalidate my claim because it is easy to tell whether one has put on one of these devices, and the user of them wants to obtain "realistic hallucinations" and so, for example, will probably avoid the kind of magnificational scrutiny that must always end by destroying the illusion.

8 J. J. Gibson, "New Reasons for Realism" (1967), reprinted in Reed and Jones, *Reasons for Realism.*

9 See Reed, *Encountering the World,* chaps. 8–11, for more details on the development of experience in a social setting.

10 For a vivid and often heartbreaking description of the lack of resources allocated to schools, see Jonathan Kozol's *Savage Inequalities* (New York: Knopf, 1993). For an excellent introduction to current attempts to turn public schools into the kind of democratic, experiential learning communities, advocated in this book, see Deborah Meier's *The Power of Their Ideas* (Boston: Beacon, 1995).

11 Jean Baudrillard, *Simulations* (New York: Semiotext[e], 1983); Paul Virilio, *War and Cinema: Logistics of Perception* (London: Verso, 1989).

CHAPTER SIX    Experience and Love of Life

1 I confess that the idea that all experience is indirect has always sounded so ridiculous to me that I have often used it as a reductio-ad-absurdam argument against the standard view of experience. But many well-known proponents of

this view emphasize just this solipsistic account of experience-as-being-out-of-touch. A good example would be Daniel Dennett, in his "Recent Work in the Philosophy of Mind," *American Philosophical Quarterly* 15 (1978): 249–263.

2  To my knowledge, this gap in Western philosophy has not been discussed seriously. Our philosophers appear uninterested in comparing the virtues of different activities or ways of life. In the Western tradition, writers on ethics tend not to consider the contrast between the pleasures of life as a voluptuary and life as, say, a carpenter. In his *Utilitarianism,* John Stuart Mill differentiated between what elite philosophers considered good and a source of pleasure, and what pigs might consider good. His theory of the greatest good for the greatest number also included the idea that the goods should be "good goods" and not just the pleasures of the pigsty. But Mill, who typically discussed all sides of an issue with considerable insight, has little to say about how one differentiates between good goods and piggish goods. In this regard, sadly, Mill does not stand much above such popular hacks as William Bennett, who in his *Book of Virtues* (New York: Simon and Schuster, 1993) simply assumes that we all know and agree about what constitutes a virtue. We must turn to creative writers for serious comparisons of different systems of value. In his masterpiece *Sacred Hunger* (New York: Norton, 1992), for example, Barry Unsworth effectively compares several of the ideal virtues of Western civilization with various alternatives.

3  For issues in translating Freud, see Bruno Bettelheim's *Freud and Man's Soul* (New York: Vintage, 1983); on "wishes" see E. B. Holt's neglected gem, *The Freudian Wish and Its Place in Ethics* (New York: Holt, 1915).

4  For Freud's relation to standard modern psychological theories, see Mary Henle's "Freud's Secret Cognitive Theories," in her *1879 and All That* (New York: Columbia University Press, 1986). The theories are not really secret: Freud was explicit about his debt to mainstream psychology as early as *The Interpretation of Dreams* (1900).

5  Sigmund Freud, *Civilization and Its Discontents* (New York: Norton, 1961); Freud, *Introductory Lectures on Psychoanalysis* (New York: Norton, 1966). For the sake of simplicity I shall not discuss Freud's third principle, the death wish, which is the subject of his *Beyond the Pleasure Principle* (New York: Liveright, 1929).

6  See E. S. Reed, *Encountering the World: Towards an Ecological Psychology* (New York: Oxford University Press, 1996), esp. chap. 9.

7  John Dewey, *Experience and Education,* reprinted in *The Later Works of John Dewey,* vol. 13 (Carbondale: Southern Illinois University Press, 1988), 11.

8  Ibid., 336.

9  Jane Healey, *Endangered Minds* (New York: Simon and Schuster, 1990), has many insights concerning the detrimental effects of poor experience. But she

is so captivated by the "stimulation" metaphor that a reader might mistake her plea for increasing *meaningful* stimulation to children with older pleas for increasing stimulation per se. For substantiation of the claim that brain growth is in part a resultant of experience, see Gerald Edelman, *Topobiology* (New York: Basic, 1988).

10 See the discussion of the importance of agency in Eleanor J. Gibson, "Has Psychology a Future?" *Psychological Science* 5 (1994): 69–76.

11 Reed, *Encountering the World,* chap. 10.

12 See Healey, *Endangered Minds.*

13 See Barbara Rogoff, *Apprenticeship in Thinking* (New York: Oxford University Press, 1990).

14 See Dewey, *Experience and Education.*

15 Ibid., 41.

16 Robert Westbrook's *John Dewey and American Democracy* (Ithaca: Cornell University Press, 1991), shows how mistaken this reading is.

17 Lewis Mumford, *The Golden Day* (New York: Liveright, 1924). For a useful contrast of Dewey and Mumford see Robert Westbrook, "Lewis Mumford, John Dewey, and the 'Pragmatic Acquiescence,' " in T. P. Hughes and A. C. Hughes, eds., *Lewis Mumford: Public Intellectual* (New York: Oxford University Press, 1990).

18 Christopher Lasch, *The Revolt of the Elites* (New York: Norton, 1995), 79.

19 Figures are from John Bellamy Foster, "Global Ecology: The Common Good," *Monthly Review* 46 (1995): 1–10.

CHAPTER SEVEN   Experience and the Birth of Hope

1 For an informed account of the economic constraints on modern work and workplace life, see Juliet Schor, "A Sustainable Economy," *Open Magazine Pamphlet Series,* no. 31 (Westfield, N.J.: Open Magazine, April 1995).

2 William James, *The Varieties of Religious Experience,* in James, *Writings, 1902–1910* (New York: Library of America, 1987).

3 William Leach, *Land of Desire: Merchants, Power, and the Rise of a New American Culture* (New York: Random House, 1993), 11.

4 Of course it is always easier to believe that our judgments are correct and "certain" if we do not open them up to public scrutiny. Could it be that one reason public discourse has grown increasingly acrimonious in recent years is that fewer and fewer people have experience with the kind of give-and-take that must occur if judgments are to be made public and evaluated?

5 See T. J. Jackson Lears, *Fables of Abundance: A Cultural History of Advertising* (New York: Basic, 1994).

6 Joan DelFattore, *What Johnny Shouldn't Read: Textbook Censorship in America*

(New Haven: Yale University Press, 1992); James W. Loewen, *Lies My Teacher Told Me* (New York: New Press, 1995).

7  Richard Rorty, *The Consequences of Pragmatism* (Minneapolis: University of Minnesota Press, 1982), 220–221.

8  Bertolt Brecht, "In Praise of Doubt," trans. Martin Esslin, in Brecht, *Poems 1913–1956* (London: Methuen, 1979), 333–336. Further quotations from the poem are from this edition.

9  Charles Taylor, *The Malaise of Modernity* (Concord, Ont.: Anansi, 1991), reprinted in the United States as *The Ethics of Authenticity* (Cambridge: Harvard University Press, 1993).

10  Paul R. Loeb, *Generation at the Crossroads* (New Brunswick, N.J.: Rutgers University Press, 1994).

11  Claes von Hofsten, "Prospective Control: A Basic Aspect of Action Development," *Human Development* 36 (1993): 253–270; Claes von Hofsten and D. N. Lee, "Dialogue on Perception and Action," in William Warren and Robert Shaw, eds., *Persistence and Change* (Hillsdale, N.J.: Erlbaum, 1985).

12  Julie Mostov, *Power, Process, and Popular Sovereignty* (Philadelphia: Temple University Press, 1992).

13  William Morris, "The English Pre-Raphaelite School," in May Morris, *Selected Speeches of William Morris* (London: Routledge, 1936).

14  William Morris, "Useful Work Versus Useless Toil," in Morris, *Signs of Change* (Bristol, Eng.: Thoemmes, 1994), 98.

15  See E. P. Thompson, *William Morris: Romantic to Revolutionary* (Stanford: Stanford University Press, 1988), and Fiona MacCarthy, *William Morris: A Life for Our Times* (New York: Knopf, 1995).

16  William Morris, "A Factory as It Might Be," in G. D. H. Cole, ed., *William Morris: Prose, Poems, Lectures, and Essays* (London: Nonesuch, 1934).

17  Christopher Lasch, *The Revolt of the Elites* (New York: Norton, 1995).

18  See Asa Briggs, introduction to William Morris, *News from Nowhere and Selected Writings and Designs* (Harmondsworth, Eng.: Penguin, 1980), 17.

19  William Morris, "How We Live and How We Might Live," in *Signs of Change,* 10.

20  William Morris, "Art and Socialism," in Morris, *Collected Works* (London: Longmans, 1936), 23:194.

21  Martin Seligman, *Learned Optimism* (New York: Knopf, 1990); Christopher Peterson, *Learned Helplessness: A Theory for the Age of Personal Control* (New York: Oxford University Press, 1993).

22  See Christopher Lasch, *The Culture of Narcissism* (New York: Norton, 1974).

23  D. Oyserman and H. R. Markus, "Possible Selves and Delinquency," *Journal of Personality and Social Psychology* 59 (1990): 112–125.

24  See C. R. Snyder et al., "The Will and the Ways: Development and Valida-
tion of an Individual-Differences Measure of Hope," *Journal of Personality and
Social Psychology* 60 (1991): 570–585.

25  Deborah Meiers, *The Power of Their Ideas* (Boston: Beacon, 1995).

EPILOGUE  Fighting for Experience

1  From a statement Picasso issued in the mid-1940s, cited in Patrick O'Brian's
fascinating *Pablo Ruiz Picasso: A Biography* (New York: Norton, 1976), 376.

2  John Dewey, *Experience and Education,* in *The Later Works of John Dewey,* vol.
13 (Carbondale: Southern Illinois University Press, 1988), 18.

3  James J. Gibson, *The Senses Considered as Perceptual Systems* (Boston:
Houghton Mifflin, 1966), 321.

# FURTHER READING

Austin, J. L. A. *Sense and Sensibilia*. New York: Oxford University Press, 1962.

Beckett, S. *I Can't Go On, I'll Go On: A Selection*. New York: Grove, 1976.

Beiser, F. *The Fate of Reason*. Cambridge: Harvard University Press, 1987.

Berry, W. *What Are People For?* San Francisco: North Point, 1990.

Braverman, H. *Labor and Monopoly Capital: The Degradation of Work in the Twentieth Century*. New York: Monthly Review Press, 1974.

Burtt, E. A. *The Metaphysical Foundations of Modern Physical Science*. Garden City, N.Y.: Doubleday, 1932.

Caton, H. *The Origin of Subjectivity*. New Haven: Yale University Press, 1973.

Cottingham, J. *Descartes*. London: Routledge, 1990.

Dennett, D. 1991. *Consciousness Explained*. Boston: Little, Brown.

Descartes, R. "The Discourse on Method" (1637). Reprinted in *Philosophical Works of René Descartes,* ed. J. Cottingham et al. New York: Cambridge University Press, 1987.

Dewey, J. *Democracy and Education*. New York: Macmillan, 1916.

——. *Experience and Education* (1938). Reprinted in *The Later Works of John Dewey,* vol. 13. Carbondale: Southern Illinois University Press, 1988.

———. *Freedom and Culture.* New York: Putnam's, 1939.

———. *Human Nature and Conduct* (1924). Reprinted in *The Middle Works of John Dewey,* vol 12. Carbondale: Southern Illinois University Press, 1988.

———. *Individualism Old and New.* New York: Putnam's, 1930.

———. *Liberalism and Social Action* (1937). Reprinted in *The Later Works of John Dewey,* vol. 11. Carbondale: University of Southern Illinois Press, 1991.

———. *The Quest for Certainty.* New York: Putnam's, 1929.

———. *Reconstruction in Philosophy.* New York: Macmillan, 1919.

Ellenberger, H. *The Discovery of the Unconscious.* New York: Basic, 1970.

Freud, S. *Beyond the Pleasure Principle.* New York: Liveright, 1928.

———. *The Interpretation of Dreams.* New York: Avon, 1965.

———. *The Psychopathology of Everyday Life.* New York: Norton, 1989.

———. *The Question of Lay Analysis.* New York: Norton, 1969.

Garson, B. *The Electronic Sweatshop.* New York: Viking, 1989.

Gay, P. *Freud: A Life.* New York: Norton, 1988.

Gellner, E. *The Devil in Modern Philosophy.* London: Routledge, 1974.

Gibson, E. J. *An Odyssey in Learning and Perception.* Cambridge, Mass.: MIT Press, 1991.

Gibson, J. J. *The Ecological Approach to Visual Perception.* Boston: Houghton Mifflin, 1979.

———. *The Senses Considered as Perceptual Systems.* Boston: Houghton Mifflin, 1966.

Grene, M. *The Knower and the Known.* Berkeley: University of California Press, 1974.

Guttman, A. *Democratic Education.* Princeton: Princeton University Press, 1992.

Healey, J. *Endangered Minds.* New York: Simon and Schuster, 1990.

Holt, E. B. *The Freudian Wish and Its Place in Ethics.* New York: Holt, 1915.

Husserl, E. *The Crisis of European Science* (1937). Evanston, Ill.: Northwestern University Press, 1970.

James, W. *Essays in Radical Empiricism* (1912). Cambridge: Harvard University Press, 1984.

Kafka, F. *The Trial.* New York: Knopf, 1964.

Kant, I. *The Critique of Pure Reason* (1781). Trans. N. Kemp Smith. New York: Macmillan, 1929.

Kenner, H. *The Mechanic Muse.* New York: Oxford University Press, 1987.

Kozol, J. *Savage Inequalities*. New York: Knopf, 1993.

Lasch, C. *The Revolt of the Elites*. New York: Norton, 1995.

———. *The True and Only Heaven*. New York: Norton, 1993.

Lehrer, K. *Thomas Reid*. New York: Routledge, 1989.

MacCarthy, F. *William Morris: A Life for Our Times*. New York: Knopf, 1995.

McDowell, J. *Mind and World*. Cambridge: Harvard University Press, 1994.

Mandelbaum, M. *History, Man, and Reason*. Baltimore: Johns Hopkins University Press, 1971.

Meiers, D. *The Power of Their Ideas*. Boston: Beacon, 1995.

Minow, N., and C. Lamay. *Abandoned in the Wasteland: Children, Television, and the First Amendment*. New York: Hill and Wang, 1995.

Morris, W. "How We Live and How We Might Live" (1888). Reprinted in *Hopes and Fears for Art and Signs of Change*. Bristol, Eng.: Thoemmes, 1994.

———. *News from Nowhere and Other Writings*. Harmondsworth, Eng.: Penguin, 1993.

———. *Selected Prose, Verse, and Lectures*. New York: Random House, 1948.

Mumford, L. *The Myth of the Machine*. New York: Harcourt, Brace, and World, 1967.

Noble, D. *Progress Without People*. Chicago: Charles Kerr, 1994.

Norton, D. *Democracy and Moral Development*. Princeton: Princeton University Press, 1991.

Pawel, E. *A Nightmare of Reason: The Life of Franz Kafka*. New York: Farrar, Straus, and Giroux, 1984.

Postman, N. *The End of Education*. New York: Knopf, 1995.

———. *Technopoly*. New York: Vintage, 1992.

Putnam, H. *Pragmatism: An Open Question*. Oxford: Basil Blackwell, 1995.

———. *Realism with a Human Face*. Cambridge: Harvard University Press, 1990.

———. *Reason, Truth, and History*. New York: Cambridge University Press, 1981.

———. *Renewing Philosophy*. Cambridge: Harvard University Press, 1992.

Reed, E. S. *Encountering the World: Towards an Ecological Psychology*. New York: Oxford University Press, 1996.

———. *From Soul to Mind: The Emergence of Psychology, 1815–1890*. New Haven: Yale University Press, forthcoming.

——. *James J. Gibson and the Psychology of Perception*. New Haven: Yale University Press, 1988.

Reid, T. *Essays on the Intellectual Powers of Man* (1785). Cambridge: MIT Press, 1969.

Rorty, R. *The Consequences of Pragmatism*. Minneapolis: University of Minnesota Press, 1982.

——. *Contingency, Irony, and Solidarity*. New York: Cambridge University Press, 1989.

——. "Dewey Between Hegel and Darwin." In *Modernist Impulses in the Human Sciences, 1870–1930,* ed. D. Ross. Baltimore: Johns Hopkins University Press, 1994.

——. *Objectivism, Relativism, and Truth*. New York: Cambridge University Press, 1991.

——. *Philosophy and the Mirror of Nature*. Princeton: Princeton University Press, 1979.

Russell, B. "Physics and Perception." In *The Analysis of Matter*. London: Allen and Unwin, 1927.

Sanders, B. *A Is for Ox: The Collapse of Literacy and the Rise in Violence*. New York: Vintage, 1994.

Schneider, H. *A History of American Philosophy*. New York: Columbia University Press, 1964.

Schopenhauer, A. *The World as Will and Representation* (1819). Trans. E. F. J. Payne. New York: Dover, 1978.

Searle, J. *Minds, Brains, and Science*. Cambridge: Harvard University Press, 1984.

Seligman, M. *Learned Optimism*. New York: Knopf, 1990.

Snyder, C. *The Psychology of Hope: You Can Get There from Here*. New York: Free Press, 1994.

Stoll, C. *Silicon Valley Snake Oil*. Garden City, N.Y.: Doubleday, 1995.

Taylor, C. "Liberal Politics and the Public Sphere." In *Philosophical Arguments*. Cambridge: Harvard University Press, 1995.

——. "Overcoming Epistemology." In *Philosophical Arguments*. Cambridge: Harvard University Press, 1995.

——. *The Sources of the Self*. Cambridge: Harvard University Press, 1989.

Thibadeau, R. *How to Tell When You're Tired*. New York: Norton, 1995.

Thompson, E. P. *William Morris: Romantic to Revolutionary*. Stanford: Stanford University Press, 1976.

Thoreau, H. D. "Civil Disobedience" (1849). Reprinted in *Civil Disobedience and Other Essays*. New York: Dover, 1993.

West, C. *The American Evasion of Philosophy: A Genealogy of Pragmatism.* Madison: University of Wisconsin Press, 1989.

Westbrook, R. *John Dewey and American Democracy.* Ithaca: Cornell University Press, 1991.

Whitehead, A. N. *Science and the Modern World.* New York: Macmillan, 1925.

Wild, J. *The Radical Empiricism of William James.* Garden City, N.Y.: Doubleday, 1969.

# INDEX

Affordances of the environment, 92–
93. *See also* Experience: as source of
meaning; Value, theories of

Appearance versus reality, 17–18, 65.
*See also* Subjectivism

Arendt, Hannah, 7, 106–107

Argyle, Michael, 82

Aristotle, 13, 37

Austin, J. L. A., 27

Authenticity, in presentation of self to
others, 139–142, 151

Autonomy, 77–78, 87, 89, 93–94, 107,
127–128, 135

Beckett, Samuel, 68–69, 72, 171n2

Beniger, James, 77

Benjamin, Walter, 81

Berry, Wendell, 130

Bloom, Allan, 76

Braverman, Harry, 7

Brecht, Bertolt, 139–141

Briggs, Asa, 152

Brokering style. *See* Experience: brokering style

Cartesian philosophy, 7–8, 10, 14–15,
24, 37, 51, 56–59, 65, 102, 136, 140.

*See also* Representational theory of
mind

Certainty, quest for, 38, 48–49, 57–59,
65, 79, 156

Competition, in a market, 65. *See also*
Division of labor

Condillac, Etienne de, 25

Daily life, 15, 22–23, 33, 46, 51, 54, 59,
66–67, 75–77, 81, 86, 88, 133–139,
145; barbarism of, 5, 35, 50, 134;
pleasure in, 123–125

Democracy, in everyday life, 6, 37, 128,
130, 145–153. *See also* Autonomy

Dennett, Daniel, 69, 88

Descartes, René, 8, 11, 14–15, 25, 52–
54, 56–57, 59, 68, 70, 99, 116. *See
also* Cartesian philosophy

Dewey, John: pragmatism of, 8, 11–12,
129–131; critique of Western tradition, 22–24, 31, 41–50; on freedom,
37–41; on promoting growth of the
self, 64, 69, 104, 125–126, 128, 133,
143; on importance of skill, 76–77;
on division of labor, 82; on community, 115, 155, 161–162

Division of labor, 80, 82–87, 90, 106.
  *See also* Work: degradation of

Ecological psychology, 7, 25, 30, 93, 99,
  116, 118, 143. *See also* Perception:
  ecological approach to
Education, 6–7, 78–79; Dewey's critique of, 7–8, 47, 126, 129, 155;
  public, 76, 128, 130–131, 133–134,
  155; funding of, 81–84, 110
Elitism, 5–6, 37, 147, 152, 159–160
Ellington, Duke, 117
Empiricism, radical, 11, 27, 165n1
Eros, 121, 123–125
Experience: secondhand, 2–4, 7–8, 33,
  75, 93–94, 106–109, 134; firsthand,
  2–4, 21, 30, 36, 42, 51, 60, 80, 93–
  94, 100, 106–109, 134, 158, 162–
  163; degradation of, 5–6, 20, 50, 52,
  59–61, 68–91, 106–109, 125, 131,
  135, 145; as source of meaning, 6, 15,
  21, 30–31, 36, 42, 47–48, 51, 80, 92,
  98, 100–102, 117, 123–124, 143–
  145, 158; respect for, 6, 38–40, 46;
  philosophical critique of, 10–11, 13,
  16–17, 21, 27–31, 50–51, 54–57,
  60–61, 93, 118, 133, 138, 170n2;
  subjective, 11–12, 56, 105; social, 41,
  62, 92–106, 114, 125, 128, 142, 155;
  learning through, 47–48, 67, 101–
  104, 107, 143–145, 155–156, 162–
  163; machining of, 62–63, 85, 90–
  91, 126, 134, 163; brokering style,
  136–139, 140, 145–147, 162. *See also*
  Senses: impressions
Exploration, of the environment, 3, 20,
  25, 30–31, 92–98, 104–106, 112–
  114, 126, 162–163. *See also* Perception: ecological approach to

Fairy tales, and philosophy, 34–35
Freedom: negative versus positive, 38–
  39, 128; nature of, 38–40, 43, 45, 47,
  68–69, 87
Freud, Sigmund, 120–121, 123, 125,
  165n1

Galileo, 14, 25
Garson, Barbara, 88–90
Geertz, Clifford, 49
Gibson, James J., 7–8, 25, 30, 92, 95,
  96, 117–118, 133, 143, 162–163
Goethe, J. W. von, 133
Good, nature of the, 43, 49, 118. *See
  also* Value, theories of
Gordon, R. B., 62
Greek philosophical tradition, 11, 13,
  37
Growth, conditions for human, 47–48,
  64, 80, 125–128, 143–145, 149, 155

Habit, 42–43
Hallucination, 27–28, 98–99, 167n21.
  *See also* Illusions, of sense experience
Hegel, Georg W. F., 17–19
Heidegger, Martin, 12, 23
Hendrix, Jimi, 21
Hobsbawm, Eric, 5
Hofsten, Claes von, 144
Hope, as sustaining human activity,
  153–157
Hume, David, 49
Huxley, Thomas Henry, 150

Idea, concept of, 13–14, 24, 57, 114.
  *See also* Senses: impressions
Illusion, argument from, 17, 54
Illusions, of sense experience, 17, 99,
  119
Impressionism, 19–20
Infancy, experience during, 111, 121–
  123, 127. *See also* Perception, development of
Information: today as age of, 1, 39, 73,
  75, 105; processed, 2–3, 59, 72–75,
  106–109, 137; ecological, 2–3, 92–
  94, 101–103, 126, 144; selection of,
  94, 107–109. *See also* Experience:
  secondhand
Information technology, 1–3, 59, 61,
  63, 71, 73, 75, 78, 172n15
Intellectuals, role of in modern world,
  6–7, 32, 47, 51, 139, 150–151

Intelligence, 71, 80
Interaction, face-to-face, 2–3, 5, 62,
    89, 101–104. *See also* Experience: so-
    cial
Invisibility, and perception, 97–98, 99–
    100

James, William, 8, 11, 12, 22, 24, 27,
    113, 133
Judgment: undermining of, 20, 52–54,
    58, 71, 74, 83, 90, 136, 142; develop-
    ment of, 39, 146–147, 152. *See also*
    Experience: degradation of

Kafka, Franz, 69
Kant, Immanuel, 16–17, 26, 49
Knowledge, versus experience, 13, 41,
    105
Kunstler, James Howard, 66

Language, development of, 127
Lasch, Christopher, 5–6, 130, 151, 160
Leach, William, 136–139, 162
Lee, David, 144
Locke, John, 24
Loeb, Paul, 141–142
Love, Freud's theory of, 122. *See also*
    Eros
Lovejoy, Arthur, 12
Lukács, Georg, 73

McDowell, John, 24
Marx, Karl, 75
Meaning, search for, 3, 69, 92, 104
Meier, Deborah, 155
Mind: versus body, 15, 28, 53–54, 56,
    121–123; unified with body, 104. *See
    also* Cartesian philosophy
Modernity, 2–4, 123, 140. *See also* Phi-
    losophy: Enlightenment
Montage, 110–112, 129. *See also* Tele-
    vision
Montaigne, Michel de, 21
Morris, William, 6, 76, 146–153, 157,
    161–162
Motivation, theories of, 119–123, 125

Müller, G. E., 29
Mumford, Lewis, 7, 61, 78, 129, 157

Newton, Isaac, 14
Noble, David, 59–60

Occlusion, of surfaces from a point of
    view, 97–100, 144–145
Optical flow, as information for the
    guidance of locomotion, 95–96, 144
Optic array, as ambient light informa-
    tion, 95–96

Paranoia, as characteristic of modern
    philosophy, 54–55, 58, 70, 114
Perception: causal theory of, 19–20,
    25–28, 37, 57–58, 93, 103; ecologi-
    cal approach to, 25, 30, 92–100,
    102–105, 112–113, 144; develop-
    ment of, 100–101, 112, 121, 125–
    127, 143, 145. *See also* Information:
    ecological
Philosophy: Western, 10–11, 13, 17,
    23, 28, 31, 37–38, 50, 105, 114, 118,
    133; common sense, 16; reconstruc-
    tion of, 22, 30–31, 44–45; goal of,
    22–23, 39, 48–49, 151; postmodern,
    23, 32–34, 41, 105, 111–115, 123;
    Enlightenment, 40–42, 47, 114; phe-
    nomenological, 59. *See also* Cartesian
    philosophy; Greek philosophical tra-
    dition
Picasso, Pablo, 160–161
Plato, 13, 37, 121
Pleasure principle, 121
Pointillism, as a way of representing the
    world, 22, 24
Pragmatism, 8, 11–12, 22, 40, 59. *See
    also* Philosophy: goal of
Prejudice, 58–59, 136
Prospective control of action, as central
    to planning and hope, 144–145
Putnam, Hilary, 23–24, 26–31, 40

Reality principle, 121
Reid, Thomas, 12, 16, 24, 26

Relativism, 23, 34–36, 39, 41–45, 49
Representational theory of mind, 41,
    43, 52–57, 112, 116
Representations, role played by, in
    mental life, 41, 65, 112, 143
Rogoff, Barbara, 80
Rorty, Richard, 12, 23–24, 32–37, 88,
    115, 150
Rosenbrock, H. H., 85
Russell, Bertrand, 12, 26

Schopenhauer, Arthur, 17–19
Scientific revolution, 10, 15, 55
Searle, John, 71–73, 78–79
Seligman, Martin, 154
Senses: impressions, 11, 19, 24, 26–27,
    29, 56, 60, 103–104, 117, 121; re-
    liability of, 11–12, 27, 56. See also
    Experience: secondhand
Sex, and experience, 4–5, 120, 123
Skepticism, 51–55, 140. See also Cer-
    tainty, quest for
Skills, significance of, 59–60, 63, 65,
    74, 76, 106–107, 124, 159. See also
    Work: good
Smith, Adam, 72–74, 106, 134
Socrates, 121, 123
Specialization, 32, 75, 77, 79–87. See
    also Division of labor
Standardization: of products, 79–84; of
    workers, 84–85, 87
Subjective versus objective world, 11,
    14, 27, 54–56, 93, 117, 121, 123

Subjectivism, 12, 15, 24, 26, 56, 13,
    113, 116–118, 120, 136, 142

Taste, relativity of, 36, 118–119
Taylor, Charles, 140, 142–143, 156,
    168n25
Technics, versus technology, 64, 78,
    107, 135
Technology, impact on work, 1, 59–60,
    73–78
Television, 5, 107–112, 131, 135
Thoreau, Henry David, 70–71, 73
Titchener, E. B., 29
Truth, 23, 105, 112–115, 118

Unconscious mental states, 19–20, 28
Utopian thought, 34–35, 43, 48, 88

Value, theories of, 36, 119, 121–123,
    139
Virtue, 3, 81, 120, 139, 175n2

Wisdom, 14, 22–23, 66–67, 81, 111,
    146
Wittgenstein, Ludwig, 13, 23
Work: mindless, 1, 51–52, 60, 62, 65,
    73–74, 80–86; degradation of, 7, 52,
    58–61, 68–91, 134, 137, 147, 170n8;
    good, 47, 76, 106–107, 113, 115,
    124, 148–149, 152
Wundt, Wilhelm, 29